To Paul
with thanks for running
the best pubs in Liverpo - L!

LIVERPOOL PUBS

With Best Wishes

KEN PYE

Ken Pye

AMBERLEY

First published 2015

Amberley Publishing
The Hill, Stroud
Gloucestershire, GL5 4EP

www.amberley-books.com

Copyright © Ken Pye, 2015

ISBN 978 1 4456 4260 4 (print)
ISBN 978 1 4456 4270 3 (ebook)

British Library Cataloguing in Publication Data.
A catalogue record for this book is available from
the British Library.

Typesetting by Amberley Publishing.
Printed in the UK.

Contents

Introduction

Sadly, the number of pubs is dwindling all across Britain as society changes, and nowhere more so than in Liverpool. The 'pub on every corner' that was once the norm in such industrialised cities and ports is certainly no longer the case, because the social function that these once provided is no longer quite as necessary. Also, it is now safe for people to drink the water! This, of course, was one reason why, during the nineteenth century, the government heavily subsidised brewers and encouraged them to build thousands of public houses.

This was to give people an alternative to drinking the often typhus and cholera-ridden water then available, as well as to get them away from drinking gin, which was almost as destructive. In fact, people were giving this to their children, largely as a very effective pacifier. This meant that there were then just as many paralytic babies and children on the streets and lying in gutters as there were adults.

It was the Prime Minister of the day, The Duke of Wellington (1769–1852), who, in 1830, passed the 'Beer House' Act. This gave permission for any householder to obtain a licence, which cost only two guineas, to sell beer from their own home. This they could either brew themselves or buy wholesale from a brewery. This was enthusiastically taken up in Liverpool, where over 20,000 private beer houses were established, almost overnight!

In due course, as we shall see in this book, from the middle decades of the nineteenth century, many such beer houses were taken over by breweries and relicensed as public houses. This was when chains of pubs, owned by individual families or companies of brewers, first began to appear, each selling their own brands of ale and, later, wines.

Nevertheless, a fair number of wonderful pubs do remain. Of these I have chosen what I consider to be the most interesting or significant for this book. However, I do recognise that this is very much a personal and subjective view, and I have had to leave some places out, but only because of limitations of space. I hope, though, that you will appreciate and enjoy reading about the ones I have been able to include, and about the neighbourhoods and communities they still serve. I hope too that if you do not already know them, you will have the opportunity to discover for yourself these fascinating and historic pubs of Liverpool city centre.

Ken Pye
Liverpool, 2015

Chapter One

The Seven Ancient Streets

Liverpool is not listed in the Domesday Book, which was produced in 1086. This was William the Conqueror's (1028–87) great ledger of all he had won after his usurpation of the English throne. This followed his victory at the Battle of Hastings in 1066. The town only came into existence in the early years of the thirteenth century, when the then King of England, John (*c.* 1166–1216), needed a north-west port from which to invade Ireland. His attention was then drawn to the great tidal pool of the hitherto obscure fishing hamlet of 'Leverpul', and he then created this as a new port, town and borough in August 1207.

As part of the establishment of the town it was ordered that seven streets be laid out to become the hub of this new community. These streets still exist, in exactly the same positions they had over 800 years ago. Taverns and inns played such a vital part in the social and economic life of the town, and its port, as it grew over the centuries, that this district of the modern city, which was once its medieval heart, seems the best place to begin a celebration of the most interesting and historically significant pubs in Liverpool.

YE HOLE IN YE WALL, 4 Hackins Hey, Liverpool, L2 2AW

Ye Hole In Ye Wall stands in one of Liverpool's few remaining medieval alleyways – Hackins Hey. This runs off Dale Street, which was one of the town's first 'seven streets'. This very quaint and cosy hostelry is claimed to be the oldest pub in the centre of the modern city, but the date of 1726, which is emblazoned on its façade, is unlikely to accurately refer to the current building, old though it certainly is.

A little further up the road, on the same side as the pub, a building was erected around 1700, which was registered as a meeting house for the Society of Friends (Quakers). This was the first place of worship in the town for this sect of dissenting Christians. On the open land adjoining this, the Quakers created a burial ground, which was in use until 1791. By this time a significant number of people had been buried there, but

Left: Ye Hole In
Ye Wall – Liverpool's
oldest pub?

Below: The cosy snugs just
off the bar.

it was in that year that the Quakers chose to leave their meeting house and graveyard, and they relocated to another part of the town.

The old meeting house then had a variety of uses, until 1813, when it became a schoolhouse. It was then demolished in 1861, and warehouses built on the site. Soon after the Quakers moved away, though, a number of dwellings and stables were built over their now disused burial ground, including in all probability the present pub. This is why Ye Hole In Ye Wall is certainly more recent that its alleged date. However, the 1726 claim possibly refers to an earlier tavern that is likely to have stood close to the Quaker meeting house. Perhaps this is why they chose to move; the consumption of alcohol was certainly not approved of by the doctrines of their faith!

So it may well be that the tavern name, rather than its building, dates from the early decades of the eighteenth century. However, it is known that the present pub is indeed standing over the Quaker cemetery. This explains two things about the pub: its ghosts, and why its cellar is actually on the upper floor with the beer being piped downstairs. The barrels have always been kept above the bar because a cellar could not be dug down into a graveyard full of corpses! Even so, the beer is perfectly refrigerated and well kept, with barrels being hoisted up from the courtyard next door. The empty ones are then dropped down again, onto large beanbags, for the draymen to carry away.

One of a few spectres that are said to haunt the pub is of a hunched and shuffling male figure, whose features cannot be seen as he wears some sort of wide brimmed hat or hood. He is often observed in or around the pub's doorway, and his presence is often felt rather than seen.

Throughout the late eighteenth and early nineteenth centuries, sailors were attracted to the many inns and taverns that existed in the streets and alleys of the old town, and not least to Ye Hole In Ye Wall because of its fine ales and welcoming barmaids. This also made the pub a regular target of the Press Gang, who were in league with the landlord.

The sole purpose of this government-sanctioned (and paid) mob of thugs was to abduct able-bodied men, especially those who clearly had experience at sea, to serve in the Royal Navy. Nobody willingly went to sea in the 'senior service', as conditions were dreadful, discipline was harsh and often fatal, and life was also frequently cut short by war. This is why the Press Gang, at best, simply surprised and overpowered their quarry or, at worst, knocked them senseless before carrying them off. Their unfortunate victims were then taken away from their homes, professions, wives, and children, often for years. That is, of course, if they ever returned at all.

Whenever the landlord of Ye Hole In Ye Wall had a 'likely' customer, especially a seafarer who was becoming drunk and insensible, he would send the pub's pot-boy to fetch the gang, who would then arrive and abduct the hapless drinker. This nefarious innkeeper, who was well paid for betraying his customers, also had another ploy. If one of his prospects looked strong enough to resist kidnap, the landlord simply, and surreptitiously, dropped a shilling into the drinker's solid pewter tankard as he was filling it with ale.

When the man drained his tankard he would see the coin, and would therefore be declared as having 'taken the King's shilling'. By default he had therefore accepted the contract and had signed up for service in the Navy. If he now resisted he could

Steve Hoy, the landlord of Ye Hole In Ye Wall.

face imprisonment or even hanging, so he had to accept his fate. This is why pewter tankards began to be made with glass bases, so that drinkers could make sure that there was no shilling waiting at the bottom to ensnare them.

Not all the customers of the pub were sailors, and by the end of the 1800s and into the twentieth century, it was catering for a more white-collar clientele who now appreciated its hearty food, fine ales and still welcoming barmaids! This continued throughout the 1960s and 1970s, when copious lunchtime food choices were displayed to happy and hungry diners on a great marble slab at the end of the bar. However, in common with almost every other city-centre pub in Liverpool, this was an exclusively male establishment (apart from its staff). In fact, this was the very last pub in Liverpool to resist the women's liberation movement, waiting until 1977 before allowing in its first female customers.

Despite its sometimes violent and macabre history, Ye Hole In Ye Wall is still an exceptionally welcoming establishment. Its comfortable, dark-brown leather seating, in homely, wood-panelled booths and snugs, and its beaten copper ornamentation, all provide the ambience necessary to qualify this as being a traditional pub. Steve Hoy, the current licensee, told me,

Nobody's ever on their own here, because there's always someone who will talk to you and make you feel at home. In fact, we always say that within a few minutes of coming into the pub we will know your name, because we ask you!

This means that, in keeping with the traditional friendliness of the city, 'You'll never walk alone' in Ye Hole In Ye Wall, which makes this a perfect place to begin any exploration of Liverpool's most interesting city-centre pubs.

The main bar of Ye Hole In Ye Wall – the ghost sometimes stands at the end!

THOMAS RIGBY'S, 23–25 Dale Street, Liverpool, L2 2EZ

Fronting Dale Street, as the entire ground floor of a broad and imposing four-storey structure, stands Thomas Rigby's. This is clearly a nineteenth-century building with an ornate rooftop balustrade that bears the name 'Rigby's Buildings', and it is Grade II listed. The outside of the pub itself has Victorian, mock-Tudor styling, and a distinctive row of peculiar gargoyles set just above its doors and windows. This is just one of many things that make the pub a popular place with real character.

Tourists and other non-locals were often deceived by a sign on the front of the building, now removed, that stated 'established in 1726' – the same date as claimed by Ye Hole In Ye Wall. While the two pubs do share an adjoining courtyard, they have no recorded historical connection. However, what is known about the Rigby's site is that a brewery stood here around the early decades of the nineteenth century. This was probably part of an earlier tavern known as The George. Could the heritage that both pubs claim originate from this old inn?

Records are unclear because tracing the history of most pubs and taverns, especially in Liverpool, is quite difficult. This is due to the fact that, before the mid-nineteenth century, they were not usually listed by the names of the premises (which changed regularly on the whim of their landlords or traditions of their customers), but only by the names of their licensees or victuallers.

What is known, however, is that Thomas Rigby (1815–86) bought the building that now bears his name sometime around 1852, when it was already known as Atherton Buildings. This had been erected on the site of The George, although parts of the old inn had been incorporated into the new structure. Rigby had bought the very large building principally because of its extensive yards and warehouse capacity at the rear, which he then used as storage and supply facilities for his rapidly expanding empire of hostelries.

Thomas Rigby was originally of very humble origins. He had come to Liverpool in 1830 from Lowton Common near Newton-le-Willows, and was an ambitious budding entrepreneur. He opened up a business in the town as a wholesale and retail wine and spirit merchant, and soon became very successful. He also went into the beer business and, before long, had acquired a large number of pubs. As his prosperity increased further, he went into local politics and became a Conservative town councillor in Liverpool.

Records show that on the ground floor of his new building was the 'Commercial Coffee House', which is likely to have been the old George tavern. Rigby immediately extended and turned this back into a pub again to add to his empire. In 1865, Rigby then replaced his pub's very plain frontage with the mock-timber-framing and eccentric plaster façade that remain today, complete with its pairs of mock-medieval grotesques. He was also a shrewd publicist, and was happy to perpetuate the name by which the rear room of his tavern had become known – 'The Nelson Room'.

He did so because of a long-recited tale that Admiral Lord Horatio Nelson (1758–1805), who was especially popular in Liverpool, had once had secret assignations with his Wirral-born mistress, Lady Emma Hamilton (1765–1815), in this room, when it was part of The George. It still bears this name today, but a letter written by the great admiral, which was displayed here for many years, has now sadly disappeared. Whether Nelson did or did not drink here, with or without Emma, this room is certainly impressive and atmospheric. With its oak-panelled walls and imposing brick fireplace one could certainly believe that the great naval hero might well have quaffed a few tankards of fine ale here.

By the middle decades of the nineteenth century, Dale Street had become the principal coaching route out of the town to most of the rest of Britain. Many taverns

The main bar of Thomas Rigby's.

on the thoroughfare, including Rigby's, were now departure and arrival points for stagecoaches with names such as Tally Ho and Rob Roy. These inns provided accommodation, warm baths, hot and tasty food, and good ales, to travellers taking long, uncomfortable, and arduous journeys on the mail and passenger coaches out of Liverpool.

Rigby's establishment catered for the wealthier classes, and for those coach passengers who could afford the higher fares to travel inside the stagecoaches. Thus protected from the elements, and from frequent sprays of mud, they could also pay for additional luxuries such as blankets and straw around their feet for warmth, and the use of binoculars. They could hire these for the journey so as to better observe the towns and countryside through which their coaches were passing. The poorer classes, who could only afford to sit on the outside of the coaches, would generally drink around the corner in Ye Hole In Ye Wall!

The pub is fortunate to retain so much of its more ancient character despite its many restorations, especially some that took place in 1922, and the most recent, in 2003, by the pub's current owners, Okell's Isle of Mann Brewery. Whatever the true, original date of Thomas Rigby's (or, indeed, that of Ye Hole In Ye Wall) may actually be, I don't think this really matters. Rigby's is an old and important pub that has been serving good ale, food, and hospitality for over 150 years, and I trust that it will continue to do so for another century, at least.

The Nelson Room – did Lord Nelson meet his mistress, Emma Hamilton, here?

THE POSTE HOUSE, 23 Cumberland Street, Liverpool, L1 6BU

The Poste House Pub is fairly tiny, but it nevertheless has a ground floor bar with a single lounge area, and a bar upstairs, also with a single (though smaller) lounge. It stands in very narrow Cumberland Street, which was once another medieval alley running off Dale Street. The building was originally a private house, probably erected around the beginning of the nineteenth century over the site of Liverpool's first Jewish cemetery. The Jewish community in the town first became established in the mid-eighteenth century, with the arrival of a handful of immigrant peddlers, probably of German extraction. Liverpool's was the first Jewish community in the north of England and, for over a century, it was the largest outside London.

So while, like Ye Hole In Ye Wall, it is believed that the bodies in the cemetery still lie beneath this pub, unlike its counterpart, The Poste House does have a traditional cellar. Even so, the belief that there are bodies beneath the pub does give rise to its own stories of haunting. The pub's most frequently manifesting spectre is the mysterious 'Woman in Black'. She makes her way down the stairs from the upper bar in full view of those present. No one knows who she is, or what her history might be, but she is thought to be one of the occupants of the cemetery. There is more than one pub in Liverpool with macabre foundations!

In 1820, the occupiers of No. 23 Cumberland Street began to sell mead to men working in all the nearby warehouses. Many of these tall and grim buildings still surround the old pub. This sweet wine became so popular that seafarers began to make their way up the hill from the river to drink here. Soon, gin was also being sold from the front room of the house, which would eventually become the main bar of the present pub.

In the early days of The Poste House the pub was patronised by a very mixed clientele. Apart from local warehousemen, it is said that, in 1846, while living in England in exile from France, Louis-Napoleon Bonaparte (1808–73) took a drink here too. Louis was the nephew and heir of Napoleon I, and sometime first President of the French Second Republic and, as Napoleon III, the Emperor of the Second French Empire. In the mid-nineteenth century also, other famous drinkers here included the writers James Thackeray, Herman Melville, and Nathaniel Hawthorne. In more recent times its illustrious customers have included Prince Philip, Bob Dylan, Debbie Harry and Noel Gallagher, to name just a few.

In 1880, Queen Victoria granted a special charter to the town, creating it 'The City of Liverpool', so now its wealth and status developed even further. It was in this year too, presumably following the granting of its licence as a public house, that the former mead and gin house now began a new life as The Wrexham House. However, it was also around this time that the pub became more colloquially known as 'The Muck Midden'!

This was because the landlord at that time had found a lucrative side-line to supplement his income. All the vehicles in Liverpool at that time were horse-drawn and, for a small fee (depending on quantity), local carriage drivers and carters began dumping all their horse manure at the back of the pub. Presumably this was cheaper than dumping it in more approved places. We must also assume that the pub landlord had a ready market for this product that made the inevitable stench worth enduring by his customers as well as himself.

Right: The Poste House.

Below: The small but cosy main bar of The Poste House.

In 1899, at the bottom of Cumberland Street and across Victoria Street, the new main post office building was opened. It was from this time that the pub became known as The New Poste House Hotel. Then, from the opening decades of the twentieth century, the small pub began serving an increasingly busy city-centre commercial district, now providing beer to a growing number of office workers rather than manual workers.

Soon, it completely transformed into a much more selective pub serving hearty lunches and ales to local businessmen and city councillors. Indeed, the running of Liverpool was frequently conducted here over foaming tankards and plates of roast beef – so no change there then!

At the end of the nineteenth century, a particular regular in The New Poste House was a wealthy Liverpool cotton-broker named James Maybrick (1838–99). This dour businessman travelled regularly between his home city of Liverpool and London, where he also had offices. He came into the pub while waiting for his train, or upon returning from a business trip to the capital. Wherever he went, Maybrick carried a small, black medical bag, in which he kept a collection of surgical instruments, being a frustrated amateur surgeon.

Because of a disturbingly frank autobiographical diary, found in 1992 and purporting to be that of Maybrick, many people now believe him to have been Jack the Ripper. Throughout 1888, a number of prostitutes were grotesquely slaughtered in the dark streets of the East End of London. However, in 1889, Maybrick was himself murdered by his wife, Florence (1862–1941), which might explain why the police never caught the vicious serial killer. Maybrick used to sit in a secluded corner of the pub, which the locals have always called 'The Royal Box'. However, another even more notorious drinker who regularly sat in this particular seat was a young Adolf Hitler (1889–1945).

Many people are now sure that the future Nazi dictator of Germany had come to Liverpool between November 1912 and April 1913 to escape conscription into the army in his homeland. Here, he stayed with his half-brother, Alois Hitler Jnr (1882–1956), and his sister-in-law, Bridgid Elizabeth Hitler, née Dowling (1891–1969). His relatives had met in Dublin, married, and moved to Liverpool in 1909. Adolph stayed with them in their flat at No. 102 Upper Stanhope Street, which runs off Princes Road in the city.

However, his miserable and bitter nature, as well as his general untidiness and limited level of personal hygiene, meant that he was an irritating and unwelcome guest. He never looked for work while in Liverpool; he simply wandered the streets of the great city, or spent his time slowly nursing pints of ale in local pubs. His favourite haunt was The New Poste House, where, apart from ordering his drinks, he avoided all contact and conversation with both staff and customers, which suited them perfectly. Following the unsavory young man's return to Germany, at the insistence of his relatives, the rest of his life story is, unfortunately, only too well known.

From the 1960s, the pub became known simply as The Poste House but was threatened with demolition when the whole area around Cumberland Street was proposed for redevelopment. It was only because of a powerful campaign, mounted by members of The Campaign for Real Ale (CAMRA), local people and loyal customers, that the pub and the street were saved. While many surrounding buildings were redeveloped, The Poste House remains as one of Liverpool's most delightful and fascinating ancient hostelries, where anyone will be only to too happy to tell you tales from its peculiar past.

THE ROSE & CROWN, 7 Cheapside, Liverpool, L2 2DY

As with so many of Liverpool's older pubs, what is now The Rose & Crown began its existence at the beginning of the nineteenth century as a beer house, located at No. 7 Cheapside. Sometime in the mid-nineteenth century this was knocked through to include the house next door when it then became a licensed pub. Cheapside is one of the oldest streets in the city, and at one time this was the only route from Dale Street through to Tithebarn Street, which is another of Liverpool's 'seven streets'.

At the corner of Cheapside once stood the town tithe barn. Here, on the Quarter Days (i.e. four times a year), the populace of the town would line up to pay over a tithe, or one-tenth, of their income, produce, or labour. This was their regular and legally enforced contribution towards the upkeep of the Church establishment and its hierarchy. However, this was not the only association that this street, or The Rose & Crown Pub, had with the Church.

In 1536, King Henry VIII (1491–1547) ordered the Dissolution of the Monasteries and changed the religion of the country to the Protestant Church of England. This began the English Reformation, but before this Britain had been a reasonably contented Catholic country. However, Roman Catholics, and any other religious dissenters and Nonconformists from the new Established Church, now became the victims of intolerance and discrimination at best, and of torture and execution at worst. Indeed, in 1593, an Act of Parliament was passed that strictly prohibited Roman Catholics from practising their faith in any form. This remained in force for almost three centuries.

Roman Catholics of the Jesuit Order had been working, largely in secret, in the Liverpool area since the seventeenth century and, in 1712, they built the town's first Roman Catholic chapel since the Reformation. A second, larger chapel was built in Liverpool in 1736, only to be demolished by a mob in 1738. This was rebuilt the following year but it had to be disguised as a warehouse. It was not until the Relief Act of 1793 that Roman Catholics began to regain their basic rights. They could now vote in elections, but not sit in Parliament. Final complete emancipation only came with the enactment of the Roman Catholic Relief Act of 1829.

By 1840, prominent Catholics in Liverpool felt that the time was right for a large, new church to be built in their town to celebrate and consolidate their faith more permanently. Typically of Scousers, the meeting to plan this took place in a pub – in fact, in The Rose & Crown! In that year, eight prominent local Roman Catholic businessmen met in the Cheapside pub to draft the following proposal: 'We the undersigned, form ourselves into a provisional committee for the formation of a society with a view to erecting a Catholic Church in Liverpool.'

As a result of this small but immensely significant meeting, in 1848, the magnificent Roman Catholic church dedicated to Saint Francis Xavier was built. Still standing at the edge of the city centre, and continuing to perform a vital role in the spiritual life of the community, the church, with its brilliantly ornate interior and tall, elegant spire, remains a stunning local landmark. This was also the first Catholic church to be built in Britain following the emancipation of the Catholics.

The current licensee of The Rose & Crown, Jimmy Williams, was eager to point out an unusual phenomenon in his modern pub. At the rear of the building, near where that momentous meeting took place, the large image of a cross appeared permanently in the

The Rose & Crown in Cheapside.

Jimmy Williams, the landlord of The Rose & Crown.

Above: The main bar.

Right: The church of Saint Francis Xavier, planned in the snug of The Rose & Crown, stands in Salisbury Street, Everton.

ceiling shortly afterwards. No amount of redecoration or repainting can obliterate this image; it always comes through!

From the beginning of the eighteenth century there were a number of cottages standing on the same side of the narrow street as the ones that would eventually become the pub. The opposite side was mostly occupied by vegetable gardens, by tanners' and skinners' yards, and by a watch factory. These were all demolished in the mid-nineteenth century and, in 1866, Liverpool's Main Bridewell was built on the site.

What is now a large Grade II listed building was once a grim place. It was constructed at a time when crime was rife in Liverpool, and it became the town centre's main lockup for more than a century. The bridewell was first used to hold petty criminals, with forty-seven cells over four floors. For most of the twentieth century it was operated by the police rather than by the prison service. However, they only used it as a holding facility for people arrested in the city, who were then to appear in the adjoining magistrates' courts. The building is constructed in very solid and thick brick, and once sat in suitably forbidding Dickensian squatness behind a tall, austere wall. However, the jail has now been converted into attractive flats for students.

Although much changed and refurbished over the years, the modern Rose & Crown pub is a comfortable and spacious place in which to while away an hour or two, just as the police officers from the gruesome bridewell, and magistrates and lawyers from the jail's adjoining law courts, did for many years.

These guardians of the law frequented the pub so often that it soon developed the local nickname of 'The Pig and Whistle'! Indeed, the police in particular drank regularly in The Rose & Crown after hours. They had their own key to the premises and would let themselves in, long after the customers had left and the landlord and his family had gone to bed for the night. When he came down again in the morning, he would find the bar needing to be thoroughly cleaned and dozens of glasses needing to be washed. Even so, there was always a long row of individual piles of coins stretching the length of the bar, as each nocturnal drinker paid his bill in full. At least the landlord was never out of pocket as a result of these constabulary congregations.

THE LION TAVERN, 67 Moorfields, Liverpool, L2 2BP

The delightful Lion Tavern stands on Tithebarn Street, at its corner with Moorfields. The current building was once only half its current size and opened as a licensed oyster bar in 1842. This served local businessmen and office workers, and then passengers using the new railway station. This had opened as Exchange station, across Tithebarn Street from the oyster bar, on 13 May 1850. The station was then the terminus for travellers to and from Preston and Manchester via Bury, Bolton, and Wigan.

Liverpool, of course, had seen the establishment of the world's first inter-city passenger railway, which began service between the town and Manchester in 1830. Within twenty years of this, railways were beginning to network across Britain, and soon across Europe, America, and the rest of the world too. Then, in 1865, the oyster bar was named as The Lion Tavern, specifically to appeal to these railway passengers. This was in tribute to what had already become a very famous Liverpool locomotive, LMR 57 *Lion*. This efficient and attractive steam engine had been built in 1838, and hauled freight and then passenger trains along the original Liverpool–Manchester railway.

The *Lion* locomotive on its plinth at Lime Street station in the 1930s.

In 1859, the locomotive was bought by the Mersey Docks and Harbour Board and served on the dockside railway system until 1871. But, from that year until 1927, when she became redundant, she simply worked as a stationary pumping engine at the graving dock at Princes Dock in Liverpool. Fortunately, she was then saved and restored by the Liverpool Engineering Society.

In the years leading up to 1941, which was the year of the May Blitz on Liverpool during the Second World War, she had been displayed on a plinth at Liverpool's main railway station at Lime Street. However, the locomotive became much more widely known when it starred as the *Titfield Thunderbolt* in the 1953 Ealing comedy of the same name. She is currently in an excellent state of preservation and maintenance, and is one of the proudest exhibits in the Museum of Liverpool at Mann Island, near the City's Pier Head waterfront.

The Lion Tavern soon became a popular place to have a drink, either before or immediately after taking a railway journey from Exchange station, and was always busy. It became even more so when, by the 1880s, the railway lines now extended to North Yorkshire and Scotland. In 1888, the original station was widened and more tracks added; the station's Grand Exchange Hotel was also built. Although the station is now no longer operating, its glorious former hotel survives and has been converted into commercial and office use. In its new capacity, the former station complex still provides The Lion with regular and loyal customers.

In 1914, a major remodelling of The Lion Tavern was carried out. This was when the then owners of the pub, the Robert Cain Brewery, extended the building through to include No. 28 Tithebarn Street, and then completely refurbished the larger premises. This included new tiling throughout, and the addition of new wall partitions with etched glass and woodwork screens. The Lion was also completely repapered with William Morris-designed wallpaper. The incredibly wealthy brewer and landlord, Robert Cain (1826–1907), will feature often in this collection of Liverpool's city-centre pubs. His influence on the drinking habits and expectations of his customers was very widely felt, not least because he owned around 200 pubs in Liverpool!

The Lion remains a beautifully maintained pub, with much of the original nineteenth- and early-twentieth-century features and styling retained, despite further remodelling in the mid-1960s and late-1970s. In fact, the original dumb waiter, used to bring oysters down from the upstairs kitchens to the bar, still survives. The spacious main public bar retains the tiled walls and panelled counter, which has a beautiful, etched-glass backing. An L-shaped corridor runs behind the bar, which itself is a separate drinking area with a sliding glass hatch to serve customers. This too has original tiling and wooden framing around the etched glass screening. This leads on to two small snugs: the news room and the lounge.

Barman Declan and a satisfied customer in the main bar.

The dome in the rear lounge.

The seating in the news room, which was originally part of the next-door building, is comfortable and well upholstered, and has an attractive mosaic floor. This was originally where poorer customers could come to read newspapers, which were then quite expensive to buy, and were provided free on a daily basis by the landlord. The small room has an imposing fireplace. With its copper hood, wooden surround, and large mirror mounted above, this dates from the 1914 remodelling.

At the rear of the pub, also off the narrow corridor, is the tiny but equally comfy lounge. There is another, similar fireplace in this room, but its most attractive feature, and one which non-regulars might often miss, is the delightful stained glass dome in the ceiling. This was another addition during The Lion's 1914 redesign.

Among the more well-known customers of The Lion can be included George Formby. He was a regular in the pub, always having a last drink there after performing in Liverpool, and before catching the train back home to Wigan. In the 1920s, the founding committee of the Liverpool Boxing Stadium met in The Lion, and one of the members of this august body was the locally renowned boxing and sporting promoter, John Best. His son, Pete (*b.* 1941), was the original Beatles drummer. He came into the Lion with his dad to drown his sorrows after being sacked by the group's manager, Brian Epstein (1934–67), with the collusion of John Lennon (1940–80) and Paul McCartney (*b.* 1942), to be replaced by Ringo Starr (*b.* 1940).

The Lion Tavern.

While Ye Hole In Ye Wall claims to be 'the oldest pub in Liverpool city centre', The Lion Tavern claims to be 'the oldest continuously serving pub in Liverpool'. Again, whatever the veracity of these claims might be, both inns are attractive, comfortable, and welcoming. The Lion is slightly larger than its near-neighbour, and has a completely different style, but both inns offer the same Scouse warmth and welcome. The Lion also has its own house beer, which is named 'The Lion Returns' and is only sold in the pub.

Another thing that makes The Lion Tavern distinctive is that if you have a particular taste in music, and providing no other customers object, you can bring along your own CDs and the very friendly bar staff will play them for you!

THE PIG & WHISTLE, Covent Garden, Liverpool, L2 8UA

The Pig & Whistle is a clean, modern, inviting and comfortable pub. It has a single bar with bench and table seating, and a medium-sized snug that looks out onto the street. The walls are decorated with sea-charts, photographs, and a variety of fascinating nautical memorabilia. Also, as is usual in Liverpool, the staff and regulars are friendly and welcoming.

The pub stands on the corner of Covent Garden and Chapel Street, which is another of Liverpool's 'seven streets'. The riverfront was once directly at the bottom of this street, and the waters washed against the wall of the old chapel that gave it its name. This meant that the pub was always close to the river, and therefore to the people whose lives depended on it – seafarers and emigrants.

The building began its life as a private dwelling, built towards the end of the eighteenth century. It may even have taken in lodgers from that time, but it was certainly a boarding house by the nineteenth century. It also operated for some time as a busy brothel. This meant that lodgers would always have someone to warm their beds and their passions overnight. In keeping with the other significant 'cottage industry' of Victorian Liverpool, the building also operated as a beer house, selling ale across its threshold probably from the early 1800s. By 1875, the building had become a licensed public house, although when and why it adopted the name of 'The Pig & Whistle' is unknown.

A wooden sign displayed on the wall of the bar states, 'Emigrants Supplied'. This once hung prominently on the outside of the pub, announcing that this was also a place where people sailing from Liverpool towards a new life could buy the food and provisions that they would not find available on board ship. These people, and their families, would be passing from the 'Old World' of Europe to the 'New World' of the Americas or Britain's expanding Empire, but only after undertaking long and frequently arduous sea voyages. Liverpool was only a staging post for these hopeful, but often also desperate, men, women, and children – a place of beginnings and of possibility. For many of its customers, The Pig & Whistle would be their last stop before leaving England forever.

Very close to the pub is the entrance to a previously long hidden, top-secret, subterranean wartime battle headquarters, which is now open to the public. Between the fall of France in 1940 and the entry of America into the war in December 1941, Britain stood virtually alone against the Nazi juggernaut that had rolled out across Europe. Liverpool was vital to the nation's survival, because it was through the port that the convoys of Allied merchant ships brought vital supplies to beleaguered Britain. Under almost constant attack, they sailed into Liverpool from America, Canada, the unconquered countries of the British Empire and, in due course, from Soviet Russia too.

Hitler was perfectly aware of our strategic position, having got to know the city and its port well, if the story of him coming here as a young man is true. He now launched a relentless campaign of submarine U-boat assaults on these convoys. Against this the Royal Navy fought a determined resistance that became known as the Battle of the Atlantic. This was the longest running campaign of the war because it lasted for the entire duration of the conflict. Nevertheless, 1,285 convoys successfully thwarted the German (and later Italian) submarines. They sailed into Liverpool, bringing with them much-needed cargoes of food, fuel, medicines, raw materials, and munitions. The largest of these convoys was made up of sixty vessels.

When war was declared in September 1939, a secret headquarters was being constructed in the basement of Derby House behind Liverpool Town Hall.

Above: The Pig & Whistle standing alone on the bomb site, with the entrance to the Western Approaches Museum in the background.

Below: The main bar of The Pig & Whistle.

The map room in the Battle of the Atlantic Museum.

Upon completion in 1941, this became the home of the Atlantic Western Approaches Command, known as 'The Fortress'. It was from here, beneath the streets of the city, that this desperate maritime conflict was fought, from 50,000 square feet of gas-proof and bomb-proof bunkers.

During the Battle of the Atlantic, despite achieving ultimate victory, the Allied losses were astronomical, with over 12.8 million tons of Allied and neutral shipping being destroyed, and the loss of over 138,000 Allied sailors' lives. The British wartime Prime Minister, Winston Churchill (1874–1965), wrote in his history of the Second World War that, 'The only thing that ever really frightened me during the War was the U-Boat peril'. It is certainly true that without our victory during the Battle of the Atlantic, and the part played in this by the port, mariners, and people of Liverpool, it is quite likely that Britain would have been defeated by the Nazis.

The Pig & Whistle is now something of a landmark, because it stands alone, on a plot of land now used as an open car park, which is one of Liverpool's last existing bomb sites. Miraculously surviving Hitler's relentless aerial bombardment of the city throughout May and June 1941, it seems to symbolise the defiance and indefatigability so typical of Liverpudlians.

Many visitors to the city, as well as locals, take a drink in the hospitable Pig & Whistle, either on their way into, or after visiting, the outstanding and moving Western Approaches Museum. Both of these experiences can help put life into perspective.

One of the North Atlantic convoys bound for Liverpool.

MA BOYLE'S OYSTER BAR, 2 Tower Gardens, Liverpool, L3 1LG

Ma Boyle's Oyster Bar first opened in Old Hall Street – another of Liverpool's seven original streets – in 1870 as an oyster bar and tavern. Seemingly named after an entirely fictitious character, in 1974 the pub closed when the business and its license transferred to its present location. On the wall of the present pub is mounted a very large and impressive sculpted commemorative plaque, which records the move. Ma Boyle's stopped serving oysters only a few years ago, because demand had fallen off as tastes changed. It retained its popular name though, and this deceptively spacious though intimate pub is now just as well known for its lunchtime servings of traditional roast meats, accompanied by its fine beers.

The pub is tucked away at the end of a short, narrow cul-de-sac that runs off Water Street – yet another of Liverpool's 'seven streets'. It sits at one corner of an early-twentieth-century office block, named Tower Building, which was built in 1908. This eccentric yet attractive, marble-clad structure was designed by local architect, Walter Aubrey Thomas (1859–1934), who also built the nearby (and much more famous) Royal Liver Building.

The pub is entered from the street through a narrow doorway, which brings you into the main bar area. As well as other seating this still has a row of tall stools facing the window and set against a marble-topped counter. It was from this that customers once ate their oysters. The bar itself is small and faces the medium-sized but comfortable snug, which is reached through a square arch and up a short set of steps.

From the bar a flight of stairs carries you past the commemorative wall plaque, down to a basement seating and dining area, off which runs the pub's cellar. It is this lower bar that is the most interesting feature of Ma Boyle's. This is because you are now standing in what was once part of the grim dungeons of the ancient fortification that once stood here – the fearsome Tower of Liverpool. It is this building that gave Thomas his inspiration for the exterior styling of his modern office block, as well as its name. This certainly does look like some kind of fin-de-siècle fortress!

Although there is absolutely no remaining evidence of the previous medieval structure in this simply decorated pub, the tower's miserable history is well-documented in city records and in a wealth of historical documents. Originally, a large, early-thirteenth-century sandstone manor house stood here on what was then still the frontage of the River Mersey (hence Water Street). In 1406, its then owner, Sir John Stanley, an ancestor of the present Earl of Derby, completely rebuilt, enlarged, fortified, and battlemented what then became the headquarters for his family in the town, and a garrison for his private troops.

He renamed the new building as 'The Tower', deliberately to strike terror in his enemies, as well as in the hearts and minds of the local, Liverpudlian townsfolk, and this worked. For centuries, its exterior walls became the scene of many public hangings. Its dungeons, including the space now occupied by Ma Boyle's, saw incarceration of men, women, and children; foul tortures; and death by starvation, disease, and simple brutality. They were also the location for more protracted forms of execution, such as 'pressing to death under stones', which could take days to kill the condemned prisoner.

This is all something to ponder on while imbibing or dining in the otherwise extremely welcoming and friendly Ma Boyle's, as is the fact that this pub too is, perhaps predictably, haunted. In fact, the narrow covered passageway that runs alongside modern Tower Building and Ma Boyle's is named Prison Weint. This once led down the side of the old prison directly to the river, and ghostly cries have also been heard in this eerie alleyway.

However, on warm and sunny days and evenings, it is a delight to take your drinks outside to tables in the street or to walk in the well-tended lawns and flowerbeds of the churchyard of Liverpool parish church. Standing right next to Tower Building and accessed through an always open gateway, this place of worship is dedicated to Our Lady and Saint Nicholas. Also known as 'The Mariners' Church', records dating from 1206 refer to an already ancient, Anglo-Saxon chapel standing on the site. Since those times, and continuing to the modern day, this is the place to which seafarers and their families come to pray for a safe voyage, and to give thanks for a safe return.

The churchyard is overlooked by a white Liver Bird (see if you can spot it), and there are a number of memorials in the garden. The most poignant of these is a commemoration of the thousands of people killed during the catastrophic bombing of Liverpool and Merseyside during the Second World War.

Above: Mark Jervis, the manager of Ma Boyle's.

Left: The original Ma Boyle's in Old Hall Street, before it relocated to Tower Building.

With its stunning views of the city's iconic waterfront buildings from the church gardens, Ma Boyle's makes for a fascinating and enjoyable outing. Particularly recommended, though, is a bowl of Ma Boyle's Scouse, which knocks oysters into a cocked hat!

THE CORNMARKET, Old Ropery, Liverpool, L2 7NT

Off Fenwick Street, tucked in the narrow street known as the Old Ropery (betraying this tiny, paved cul-de-sac's former function), stands The Cornmarket pub. This is the last of the pubs in this section and it is a beautiful character tavern. It is laid out and decorated in a traditional style, with a long bar, comfortable snugs and lounges, and an interesting history.

Records indicate that beer was being sold from the premises from around 1792 and the current licensee, Kevin Smith, thinks that this too was another of Liverpool's thousands of beer houses. Records also confirm that, in the early years of the nineteenth century, what is now the rear half of the modern Cornmarket pub had already opened as The Bull's Head Tavern. This had its entrance in Moor Street, which currently runs adjacent to The Old Ropery and was another of old Liverpool town's earliest streets. Some time later, what is now the front half of the pub, with its entrance in the Old Ropery, opened as the entirely separate Cornmarket pub.

Trading in corn began in the first corn market building, which opened in nearby Brunswick Street, in 1818, so it would have been after this date that the pub opened, taking the name of this important new building. However, in 1854, the old market was replaced by a new corn exchange building, standing next to The Old Ropery, in Fenwick Street. As mentioned previously, because of the uncertain records of pub names, this means that The Cornmarket may not have opened until this later date. Nevertheless, these two popular and busy taverns remained separate until the late 1960s, when they were knocked together to become the single pub that we have today.

The pub itself adjoins the rear of Britannia Buildings, which faces on to Fenwick Street, and Kevin believes that his building was once part of that structure. Little is known about the history of Britannia Buildings except that, during the late eighteenth and early nineteenth centuries, it was once home to a small school for young ladies. Another legend associated with Lord Nelson's mistress, Emma Hamilton, is that she was a pupil here as a small child, when she was plain Emily Lyon from Neston.

Like The Pig & Whistle, The Cornmarket unbelievably avoided being destroyed in the intensive German bombing of the May Blitz in 1941, which all but levelled the centre of Liverpool. 'Blitz' is short for *Blitzkrieg* or 'Lightning War', and was the name the Hitler gave to one of his most devastating modes of warfare – his bombing of ports, towns, and cities. Many places suffered under these callous aerial assaults, but few more so than the streets, docks, canals, railways, warehouses, factories, and shipyards of Merseyside.

These attacks were first launched against the City of Liverpool during the nights of 1 to 8 May 1941. This was the worst week of sustained raids on any part of Britain, and was an all-or-nothing attempt by the Germans to wreck the port from which the Western Approaches were being defended. In just that single week, 1,453 people were killed and around 1,000 seriously injured. After this, the Nazis continued to bomb

Above: The front half of the main lounge, showing the fireplace and paneling from the *Reina del Pacífico*.

Left: Kev Smith, the licensee of The Cornmarket.

Liverpool almost every night during the remainder of May, and throughout the first two weeks of June.

Altogether, there were seventy-nine separate air raids during the Liverpool Blitz, and it was estimated that, out of the almost 300,000 homes in the city at that time, around 200,000 were damaged and 11,000 destroyed. By the end of the bombing more than 4,000 people had been killed and well over 10,000 injured. Indeed, in sheer tonnage of high explosive and incendiary bombs, Liverpool was the most heavily bombed city in Britain outside London.

Not only did The Cornmarket survive the Blitz, but it was completely refurbished and tastefully redecorated after the war. In fact, the glorious carved fireplace and wooden panelling in the main lounge of the pub were taken from the RMMV *Reina del Pacífico* passenger ship of the Pacific Steam Navigation Co. She had been launched in 1930 and was the largest, most luxurious, and fastest motor liner of her time. She sailed regularly between Liverpool and the Caribbean, through the Panama Canal, and to South America.

She was scrapped in 1958 and some of her woodwork found its way into the pub. It is unlikely that the panelling was originally carved for the ship itself and is believed to have been originally salvaged from a grand mansion house. However, from which country is uncertain, as the principal figures on the fireplace appear to be dressed in Spanish costume dating from the seventeenth century. However, this is just as likely to be a Victorian replica as a Tudor original.

Today, The Cornmarket is popular with local businesspeople and office workers during the day, and also high court judges, solicitors, and barristers from the nearby Queen Elizabeth II Law Courts. It is also a favourite watering hole and tourist attraction at evenings and weekends. It seems to have been discovered, in particular, by the Japanese, who have been mysteriously drawn to the pub. For the past fourteen years, The Cornmarket has been a featured stop on their walking tours of the city centre. In 2014 alone, over 4,000 Japanese tourists visited the pub, and most of them apparently insist on having their picture taken standing behind the bar. A troop of around twenty tourists came into the pub while I was doing my research. I was very happy to join Kev and his staff as they bade these people welcome to Liverpool, and to the impressive Cornmarket.

Chapter Two

The Cavern Quarter

Most of the streets that now form the 'Cavern Quarter' were first laid out from around 1722. This was on land then leased from the Lord of the Manor, Lord Molyneux, by John Button, who was an important and wealthy local figure in the town. Mathew Street, at the heart of the Quarter, leads into Rainford Gardens, which then connects with Button Street, which is named after John.

This compact district was first one of comfortable private dwellings, stables, and small gardens. These were soon replaced, however, throughout the nineteenth century, by tall, densely packed warehouses and offices servicing the economy of the Industrial Revolution, and many of these buildings survive.

Of course, the reason this area of the city has been given its current name is in tribute to four of Liverpool's most significant citizens: Paul McCartney, John Lennon, Ringo Starr, and George Harrison – The Beatles. Here you will find many specialist shops and bars, each one celebrating the Fab Four in its own way.

THE CAVERN, Mathew St, Liverpool, L2 6RE

I make no apology for including The Cavern in this collection, even though some might argue that it is not strictly a pub. My response is simply that the bar in The Cavern is there even when there are no live bands playing and, in its current incarnation, this is at the core of the place. Indeed, the thousands of tourists and locals who come here every week, during daytime as well as at night, will agree. There are other bars and pubs on Mathew Street, but only one other, which we shall come to next, matches The Cavern's bar in terms of iconic as well as historic significance.

Undoubtedly, The Cavern is the most important pub or club to visit in the Quarter, and it still sits deep below Mathew Street. The entrance is opposite the Liverpool Pop Music Wall of Fame, which commemorates every Number 1 Hit Record ever produced by Liverpool groups and singers. This also points out that Liverpool has more of these to its credit than anywhere else in the world!

Arguably, the original Cavern Club, which stood here at what was then No. 10 Mathew Street, was the most famous beat club in the world. However, it opened first as a jazz club on 16 January 1957, when it was the haunt of Beatniks. By 1960, live country and western music was being performed here alongside the jazz sessions; there were no discos or DJs in those days! Around this time, the skiffle craze was in full swing, following the example of Lonnie Donegan, and this gave birth to the boom in amateur and semi-professional 'skiffle groups' all over Merseyside. One of these was The Quarrymen, of which John Lennon was a founder member, and they first played at the Cavern in August 1957.

Soon, skiffle transposed into rhythm and blues, and then into beat music and early British rock 'n' roll. The Quarrymen transposed too, into the Silver Beatles, and then into The Beatles. It was on 17 February 1961 that John Lennon and The Beatles first performed at The Cavern, with Pete Best as drummer, and with Paul McCartney and George Harrison completing the 'Beat Combo'. The Cavern then became the inspiration for many groups and solo performers throughout the 1960s, and The Beatles played 275 performances there in just two years, the last being on 3 August 1963. They then went on to international stardom.

The original Cavern closed in 1973, and the cellar club was filled in in 1981, when the warehouse above it was demolished. There was a subsequent incarnation of The Cavern just across Mathew Street, but the original Cavern Club was excavated and rebuilt on its home site in 1984. In fact, local architect David Backhouse was responsible for the reclamation, during which he discovered a brick wall of arches from the rear wall of the old club, with all the band's names still painted on it. He saved these bricks and the wall, and now 85 per cent of the reconstructed club is built on the original site, using 15,000 of the original bricks. Indeed, one of the best features of the modern Cavern is the accurate reconstruction

Above right: The entrance to Liverpool's world famous Cavern.

Right: The steps wind down to the deep cellar club and bar.

Above: The Cavern bar.

Left: The reconstructed stage that has seen the world's greatest performers appear here.

of the stage on which The Beatles and so many other famous performers appeared throughout three decades.

Towards the end of Mathew Street, on the right, is the Cavern Wall of Fame. This records the name of every artist or group that appeared at the original Cavern Club, from its first opening. Each name is inscribed into an individual brick. These performers include Stevie Wonder, The Who, Gene Vincent, Little Richard, and The Rolling Stones, among so many more.

Today, The Cavern and the Quarter are a place of pilgrimage for tourists from all over the world. Every day they are seen taking dozens of photos as they try to capture for themselves just a part of this very special place in the history of twentieth-century popular music. The new Cavern Club and Bar has all the atmosphere of the original venue and a visit here, whether or not you take a drink, is certainly a powerful experience.

THE GRAPES, 25 Mathew St, Liverpool, L2 6RE

At the bottom of Mathew Street, on the opposite side to the Cavern, stands The Grapes pub. This well-kept, flower-bedecked hostelry is another popular tourist destination in the Quarter, because of its association with The Beatles. However, when it first opened as a public house in the 1850s, it was known as Commercial House. Then, in the 1870s, it became The Commercial Hotel; in the 1880s, The Letters; for two years in the 1890s, it was known as Ye Old Welsh Ale Stores; and, from 1898, as The Grapes.

Throughout the first half of the twentieth century, the pub served the warehousemen and deliverymen who worked for the many companies that operated in the district. However, in the 1950s and 1960s, Liverpool began to go into a massive economic decline as a port. The global maritime industry was changing out of all recognition and the city was failing to keep pace. Unemployment rocketed, and the once-thriving warehouses in places like Mathew Street began to close and fall derelict. However, this was also the age of 'the teenager', and the empty warehouses now became drinking dens and live music venues for this energetic generation. The Grapes changed too, as the older teenagers made it their pub of choice.

This was because clubs like The Cavern did not have alcohol licenses and only served coffee or Coca-Cola so, before and after their performances, The Beatles drank in The Grapes with fellow musicians and audience members alike. Although redecorated since those heady rock 'n' roll days, the pub remains largely unaltered from that time. Inside it is large, with a low, beamed ceiling, lots of dark wooden panelling, and leather seating, and there is 1960s Mersey Sound memorabilia throughout the pub. Some of its most fascinating decorations are the 'family trees' of Liverpool rock bands that played at The Cavern, which are painted on the walls. On a specially illustrated wallboard can also be read the story of 'The Man in the Iron Tube'. This is a pub where you can get a history lesson as well as a drink!

On either side of the single central bar there are large lounge areas with smaller snugs leading off. However, it is the rear lounge that attracts most interest, as this is where The Beatles regularly drank. A plaque marks this and a photograph on the wall shows them in their favourite seat. In the picture they are the 'pre-Fab Four', as

The famous Grapes, standing at the bottom of Mathew Street.

The main bar.

it shows John, Paul, George, and the group's original drummer, Pete Best. It was to The Grapes that Pete went, with The Beatles' roadie, Neil Aspinall, after he had just been sacked by Brian Epstein and replaced with Ringo Starr.

Almost opposite The Grapes is an Irish-themed pub called Flanagan's Apple. Set into its wall is a plaster bust of the Swiss psychologist, Carl Gustav Jung (1875–1961). He believed that most human actions are affected by the accumulation of the experiences of our ancestors, and by our own dreams and innate psyches. Jung, who never actually visited Liverpool, had a dream about the city in 1927. This had a profound effect on him and, in his book *Memories, Dreams, Reflections*, he recounts the dream, and analyses it by saying,

> I found myself in a dirty, sooty city. It was night, and winter, and dark, and raining. I was in Liverpool. I walked through the dark streets … found a broad square, dimly illuminated by street lights, into which many streets converged.
>
> … In the centre was a round pool, and in the middle of it a small island. While everything round about was obscured by rain, fog, smoke and dimly-lit darkness, the little island blazed with sunlight. On it stood a single tree, a Magnolia, in a shower of reddish blossoms. It was as though the tree stood in the sunlight and was at the same time the source of the light.
>
> … I had a vision of unearthly beauty, and that was why I was able to live at all. Liverpool is the 'pool of life'.

The rear lounge of The Grapes, which was The Beatles' favourite place in the pub.

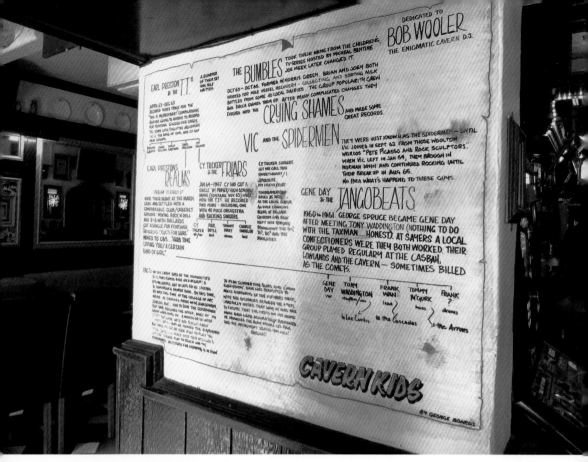

'Cavern Kids' family tree.

When the influential Beat poet, Allen Ginsberg (1926–97), visited Liverpool, the Cavern Club, and The Grapes in 1965, he came to see for himself why the world was paying so much attention to the smoky urban city on the Mersey. He was overwhelmed by what he discovered, and went on to describe Liverpool as 'the centre of the consciousness of the human universe'.

On the face of it this could be said to be a somewhat grandiose statement to make, but, when one actually considers the international cultural influence that Liverpool had at that time, then perhaps he was correct. Indeed, everything about the Cavern Quarter and The Grapes, proves that the city and the Mersey Sound continue to resonate and have impact around the world.

THE WHITE STAR, 2–4 Rainford Gardens, Liverpool, L2 6PT

The White Star stands in Rainford Gardens, just around the corner from The Grapes, yet it is still very much part of the Cavern Quarter. What is now a haven of convivial Scouse hospitality originally opened as a ships' chandlers' store in 1760, when it then stood adjacent to a very large stable yard. This regularly accommodated up to 100 horses at a time to service the Bates Hotel, which then occupied a prominent

Landlady Jackie, and John, one of the pub's regulars, in the main bar.

position on nearby Lord Street. At the end of the seventeenth century, this street had been laid out by Lord Molyneux and named after him.

The chandlery closed around 1850, when the building became a restaurant, serving the wealthier classes of Liverpool. On the top floor was the accommodation for the twelve chefs who prepared the food. In the main beams of the ceiling here can still be seen the meat hooks for the animal carcasses. Presumably these cooks shared their bedrooms with the bodies!

In 1878, the Charrington Brewery acquired the building and converted it into a public house. They completely redesigned and refitted the pub, complete with its surviving etched glass screens. They also renamed it 'The White Star' after the famous shipping line.

This company had been founded in Liverpool in 1870, first under the name of the Oceanic Steam Navigation Co. The most famous vessel in the White Star fleet was RMS *Titanic*, which is portrayed on the pub's sign and in many other photos and paintings around the premises. Indeed, the walls are covered with all kinds of memorabilia, but especially objects associated with White Star. It is always *Titanic* though, and her tragic fate, that captures the imagination of the pub's newer customers.

The White Star.

What was then the most luxurious, largest, and technologically sophisticated passenger liner of the age, set sail from Southampton on 11 April 1912, on her maiden voyage to New York, carrying 2,223 passengers and crew. Owing to a combination of bad judgement, flawed design, arrogance, and class-ridden complacency, she never reached her destination. At 11.40 p.m. on Sunday 14 April, in clear, fine weather, and on an almost dead calm ocean, she struck an iceberg. By 2.20 a.m. on 15 April, *Titanic* had sunk, with the loss of 1,157 men, women, children, and babies.

One of the pub's largest pictures of the great ship is framed and mounted on the ceiling of the smallest snug. Barman Tony Evans told me that this was so that any drunks who ended up on the floor would be forced to contemplate the results of complacent and self-indulgent excess!

Like The Grapes, The White Star grew in popularity and served the commercial and warehouse community of the neighbourhood. The pub was particularly popular with the workmen from the nearby Fruit Exchange. In the decades after the Second World

The main lounge at the rear of the pub.

War it became known locally as 'The Onion Bar', because it was here that the men came every Friday night to receive their wages. Although The White Star also fell prey to the city's post-war economic decline, it gained a new lease of life with the advent of rock music.

Not an obvious part of the Mersey music scene, in fact, the rear lounge of The White Star was used by Bob Wooler (1932–2002), the first and longest-standing compère of The Cavern, and Alan Williams (b. 1930), the first manager of The Beatles, before he sold them to Brian Epstein. From here these impresarios paid all their groups and singers, including the world famous 'Mersey Mop-Tops', and a brass plaque on the wall marks this.

Although much has remained the same in the pub since the 1960s, fortunately, other things have changed – not least the toilet arrangements! Originally, when male drinkers needed to relieve themselves, they simply did so in the open yard at the rear of the pub,

The 'Impresario's Corner' in the rear snug of The White Star.

in all weathers. Women's toilets were not installed until 1987, which is why they are upstairs. This was because of the high level of prostitution that had always existed in the city centre, so unaccompanied women were not welcome in pubs until that exceptionally late date. That is, of course, unless the landlord encouraged the women in their profession and took a cut from their earnings. I am assured that this was never the case in The White Star, though.

During the course of my exhaustive researches for this book I was made very welcome wherever I went in the city, but nowhere more so than by the customers of The White Star, and by its licencees, Alfie and Jackie Buxton. To experience true Scouse hospitality, sharp humour, and genuine good companionship, this is the place to go!

Chapter Three

Sailor Town

The part of Liverpool covered by the next section of this book was once notorious as 'Sailor Town'. This was the maritime heart of the old town and its rapidly growing port, especially throughout the eighteenth and early nineteenth centuries.

It was its docks that made Liverpool great and the world centre of maritime commerce for over 250 years. The first of Liverpool's docks was the Old Dock, which opened in 1715. This was also the world's first commercial, enclosed, wet dock, and Liverpool had docks almost fifty years before anywhere else. Indeed, London did not build its first dock until 1820.

The streets and alleyways of Sailor Town grew around the Old Dock, eventually covering an area of some 22 acres. It was bounded by Paradise and Hanover Streets, Lord Street and James Street, and by The Strand and Canning Place. Throughout the eighteenth century in particular, this was a densely packed and heavily populated area of around fifty inns and taverns. There were also dozens of tawdry lodgings and bath houses, barbers and tattooists, warehouses, sail and rope-makers, ships stores, and workshops. This district was also very well supplied with dance halls, freak shows, fortune tellers and, of course, brothels.

Mariners of every shape, size, skin colour, and language mixed freely, and in the kind of companionship that comes from being a member of a community that encompasses the world – the community of the sea. Of course, fist fights were frequent, and drunkenness commonplace, because the life of a sailor, especially during that period, was a difficult one. Indeed, violence was rife and life was cheap. However, the Old Dock and Sailor Town have long gone, and the entire area is now largely covered by the modern Liverpool ONE retail and leisure complex. Even so, there are remnants of Sailor Town in some of its few surviving pubs.

LIVERPOOL ONE BRIDEWELL, 1 Campbell Square, Argyle Street, Liverpool, L1 5FB

Built around 1850, what is now an attractive and sympathetically redesigned Grade II listed bar and restaurant was originally a police station and prison. Indeed, the old cells remain as the snugs in the modern pub.

The Argyle Street Bridewell as it looked in the 1970s.

When it was constructed, the Bridewell stood right on the edge of the docks and was surrounded by rope works and huge warehouses, many of which survive. It was opened to police the squalid and often violent alleyways and wharfsides of Sailor Town. This meant that raw Liverpool life swilled around the building, requiring a particularly hardened type of police officer. This was why, in 1860, the great Victorian writer, Charles Dickens (1812–70), chose to volunteer at the Bridewell as a special constable, to undertake truly authentic research for his books.

Dickens loved Liverpool, saying, 'Liverpool lives in my heart second only to London', and he came here regularly to give public readings of his works, as well as for his research. However, when he signed on at Argyle Street this was only for a single day. Perhaps this was all he needed, or perhaps it was all that he could take!

By the beginning of the nineteenth century, the population of Liverpool had risen to 77,653 but, if the average number of seafarers in port was added to this, together with the number of other transient workers, then the figure would be nearer 90,000. By 1800, there were five large wet docks at the centre of Sailor Town, and this number increased rapidly during the remainder of the century. Liverpool's dockland was a thriving maelstrom of life and living, as seamen spent their pay and indulged every appetite, ready to take to the seas again on voyages that might last for years before they would see their homes again – that is if they had homes. This meant that the police officers from the Argyle Street Bridewell had their work cut out, and their prison cells were always full.

The Liverpool ONE Bridewell today.

The design of the Bridewell was quite innovative for the time, because the cells were originally built to accommodate only single prisoners. Each was ventilated through a special grill, to which fresh air was fed through a system of specially designed pipes and shafts. In fact, the shafts remain, and are one of the reasons for the building's listed status. That said, demand for accommodation in the cells could reach a peak on Saturday nights, meaning that up to twenty men could then occupy a single cell. All the prisoners would have been drunk, and most of them fighting each other too, in what had now become very confined spaces. So, with what can only be described as 'do it yourself' sanitation facilities, ventilation in the cells would have been both necessary and welcome!

The modern pub is quite haunted and a number of spirits (other than the bottled variety) can sometimes be seen flitting around the building. Ghosts can also be heard moaning, whispering, and also slamming cell doors, which is a very difficult thing to do because these are so heavy! The manager of the Bridewell, Paul Fitzgerald, who was originally very skeptical when it came to all things spectral, has now changed his perspective completely since hearing his name being called by a woman's voice, in an Irish accent, from a completely empty cell and in an otherwise empty building.

The police moved out of the Bridewell in the 1930s. At the outbreak of the Second World War, it was loaned to the military, who later used it to accommodate German prisoners of war. Conscientious objectors were also held in the old prison, and it was at this time that cisterns with flushing lavatories were installed in the cells, but these have all now been removed (except in the modern toilets, of course).

The Bridewell was handed back to the police at the end of the war, who then simply used is as a storage warehouse until the 1970s. Sometime later they sold the building, which then had a number of uses. It was also closed up and derelict for a time but, in the early 1980s, it was reopened as rehearsal rooms for local musicians and groups. In fact, Liverpool bands who became successful and popular around that time, and who used the Bridewell, included The Icicle Works and Frankie Goes to Hollywood.

When Holly Johnson and his friends first formed this latter group, they rehearsed and wrote songs in the cell that is now the pub's gents' toilets! They also found the cell walls to be covered in very coarse and abusive anti-Churchill graffiti. As this was written in English, it must have been authored by the conscientious objectors rather than by the Germans. The writing on these particular walls, though, has since been painted over.

In 2003, the old prison was bought by local screenwriter and film producer Colin McKeown, who then completely restored and refurbished the building, and opened it up as a pub and restaurant. This is now one of the most popular venues in the city for locals and tourists alike, both as a place to drink and eat very well (in the cells as well as in the former officers' quarters on the upper floor), and as one of Liverpool's most unusual and historically significant pubs.

THE PUMP HOUSE, Albert Dock, Liverpool, L3 4AN

The Pump House is the next pub in this section, and is another conversion of a much older building. As its name suggests, it was originally built as the home for a great steam engine that formed part of a major technological redevelopment that took place throughout the dock network in the mid-nineteenth century. This saw the previously man-powered and horse-driven handling mechanisms replaced by automated, steam-powered hydraulic systems.

The dock that The Pump House overlooks was the port's second. This had originally been opened, in 1737, as an anchorage and entrance to the Old Dock. Three graving docks were added in 1765, and it was gated as a wet dock in 1829, being renamed as Canning Dock in 1832. Liverpool's third dock stands to the south of The Pump House and facing the Albert Dock Warehouses. This is the Salthouse Dock, which opened in 1753, and was originally named South Dock. However, it is undoubtedly the Albert Dock itself, and the attractions that now fill its remarkable surrounding warehouses, that most of the customers of the modern Pump House pub come to the waterfront to see.

Liverpool's great dock engineer and architect, Jesse Hartley (1780–1860), designed this spectacular complex, and it was the world's first fully enclosed, complete dock and hydraulic cargo-handling system. Previously, goods had been temporarily stored in wooden sheds at the docksides, and these were always at risk from fire. The Albert Dock warehouse system was the first to be built entirely of incombustible materials. Hartley's revolutionary design comprised a cast-iron, stone, and brick structure, with an innovative, stressed-skin, galvanised iron roof.

In 1846, the dock was officially opened by Prince Albert (1819–61), the Royal Consort of Queen Victoria (1819–1901), and it was named after him. At the ceremony, he said, 'I have heard of the greatness of Liverpool but the reality far surpasses the expectation.'

The Pump House viewed from Canning Dock, with the former dock traffic office and the Albert Dock warehouses behind.

The Pump House.

The warehouse buildings around the new dock made the loading and unloading of vessels a very rapid and efficient process, aided by mechanical lifting and handling devices. Goods unloaded, stored, and then shipped out again from Albert Dock included plant products like hemp, cotton, sugar, and jute. These were seasonal, so merchants could store them in the warehouses and then distribute them gradually throughout the year, thus maintaining a consistent income stream. Also, because of the secure nature of the facilities, the Albert Dock warehouses proved ideal for storage of very valuable cargoes, such as brandy, tea, cotton, silk, tobacco and sugar.

Diagonally across from The Pump House stands the striking former dock traffic office, which was designed and built between 1846 and 1847, also by Hartley. With its amazing cast-iron Tuscan portico and frieze, it was from here that the entire use and management of Albert Dock was directed. However, all of Liverpool's docks began to decline and close, especially from the 1970s. But then, from the early 2000s, it was this stretch of waterfront that became the foundation of Liverpool's cultural and economic renaissance. All the docks, warehouses, and buildings that had by then become derelict and useless were completely salvaged, restored, and re-established. This included The Pump House, the tall chimney of which had been dangerously near collapse. Now, instead of servicing cargo and commodities, these buildings catered for the tourism, leisure, retail, and entertainment sectors.

The Pump House as it looked in the late nineteenth century, when it drove all the hydraulics for the dock.

The main bar of the modern Pump House.

In more recent years, the dock traffic office became local studios for Granada Television, but it is now home to the International Slavery Museum. This is an outstanding, but nonetheless disturbingly vivid, exploration of the transatlantic slave trade, in which Britain, but especially Liverpool, played a leading role for over 100 years. The dock buildings adjacent to The Pump House also contain the very large Merseyside Maritime Museum. This explores the more pleasant, though very exciting, story of Liverpool's seafaring life and history. Both museums are internationally recognised, not just for their exhibitions and displays, but also for their archives and research facilities.

Inside what itself is a beautiful Victorian structure, with its solid but stylish nineteenth-century design, The Pump House now serves food and drink in thoroughly contemporary surroundings. Where once great machines thumped, churned, and drove an industry, now tourists and locals relax as part of their visit to Liverpool's outstanding restored docklands. The Pump House bridges the centuries, and provides a busy and entertaining link between Liverpool's old Sailor Town and the thriving, twenty-first-century waterfront of this reborn world-class city.

THE BALTIC FLEET, 33A Wapping, Liverpool, L1 8DQ

There is some evidence that a tavern of some kind has been on or very near the site of the present Baltic Fleet pub from the very early eighteenth century, possibly known by the same name. Today, however, this is now one of the last surviving of hundreds of original taverns and drinking houses that used to exist in Sailor Town.

The Baltic Fleet was once packed with sailors, warehousemen, and dockers, as well as with office workers from the surrounding district. In its current building, which is now Grade II listed, this has been a popular drinking house since the mid-nineteenth century. The pub took its name from the fleets of ships that sailed from the port to trade with the Scandinavian countries around the Baltic Sea. It also served the fearless men who sailed in the fleet of whaling ships that once left Liverpool for those cold, northern waters, as well as for Greenland and the Arctic.

From around 1750 until the early decades of the nineteenth century, whaling was a vital part of the maritime economy of the port. However, not all the trips into these icy waters resulted in successful hunts and profitable voyages and, in 1789, four whaling ships from Liverpool were lost at sea with all hands. Nevertheless, until the 1820s, whalers operated with some success.

Landlord and owner, Simon Holt, proudly stands outside The Baltic Fleet.

However, the industry had reached its peak by 1788, when twenty-one vessels were registered in Liverpool as whalers and, though the risks were high, the trade could be extremely profitable. The last permanent whaler operating out of the Port of Liverpool appears to have been a ship named the *Baffin*. This had also been the first whaling ship to be actually built in the port, in 1820, by William Scoresby. His son, William Scoresby Jnr, set sail in the summer of 1822 on a scientific voyage to Greenland. He reported his findings in a book regarded as scientifically important, entitled, *A Journal of the Voyage to the Northern Whale Fishery, including Researches and Discoveries on the East Coast of West Greenland made in the Summer of 1822 in the ship the Baffin of Liverpool*.

Nevertheless, despite Scoresby's valuable research, whaling as an industry had declined during this period and by 1827 only the *Baffin* was working as a full-time whaling ship from Liverpool. Even so, Herman Melville (1819–91), the American author, visited Liverpool in 1839, and was so inspired by the wonders of the port and by William Scoresby's book that he went on to write his great novel about whaling, *Moby Dick*, in 1851. Melville also wrote extensively about Sailor Town so is quite likely to have visited the Baltic Fleet.

The deep cellars beneath the Baltic Fleet are full of tunnels, passageways and strange hiding spaces. In fact, one of these was definitely used by sailors drinking in the pub when the 'crimps' were around. Whenever this particular type of thug was seen to be approaching the pub, weaker or already drunken men would be carried down to the safe hiding places in the cellars by their more sober fellow drinkers or by the landlord.

Whereas the Press Gang, which operated only until the mid-nineteenth century, would abduct the unwary into the Royal Navy, crimps would 'shanghai' a man into

One of the tunnels leading from the pub cellar.

forced servitude aboard merchant ships and privateers. This would be mostly on voyages to the South China Seas, hence the term. This practice developed in the latter decades of the 1800s and survived until the outbreak of the First World War.

A crimp would trick a sailor into signing up for such a long and uncertain voyage using coercion, bribery, intimidation, and violence, or by serving him a drugged drink known as a 'Mickey Finn'. In fact, this was the favoured method used by crimps, who would forge the signature of the drugged man and then carry him on board the ship. Here, the villain would be paid off by the ship's master in what was known as 'blood money'. Once on board ship, the sailor was legally obliged to fulfill the contract otherwise he would go to prison, probably for longer than he would be at sea.

The tunnels that still run from beneath the Baltic Fleet lead in a number of directions. One still goes towards the river and is thought to have been used by smugglers bringing illegal consignments of rum and tobacco ashore. A second tunnel is said to have provided direct, two-way traffic between the pub and the more popular brothels and boarding houses. This must have been very convenient for both establishments.

The present Baltic Fleet pub had a chequered history in the 1970s and 80s, opening and closing a number of times as the economy of Liverpool began to collapse. However, with a dream and an abundance of determination, the pub was bought by Simon Holt, a relative of the famous ship-owning Holt family of the city. With his family's spirit of true Scouse entrepreneurship, he plans to continue the restoration of his important pub. This includes the excavation of his mysterious tunnels and hideaways that he hopes one day to be able to open to the public.

The main bar.

The Baltic Fleet standing on Wapping.

In 2002, Simon began brewing his own ale in his cellar, with his own Wapping Beers branding. The Baltic Fleet is the only pub in Liverpool to have its own microbrewery and bottling plant on the premises, and these are helping to make the pub a very popular enterprise.

With its large bar area and home-brewed ales, and with the many nooks and snugs in which to drink them, as well as with the roaring open fire and very friendly staff and customers, the Baltic Fleet is a gem on Liverpool's historic dockland waterfront, and a growing tourist destination in its own right.

THE MONRO, 92 Duke Street, Liverpool, L1 5AG

The Monro stands on Duke Street, in what was built sometime around 1764 as a grand town house for a wealthy merchant. It was also one of the first properties on what was then a new thoroughfare. The building's main beams and floors came from decommissioned or wrecked sailing ships of the late seventeenth and early eighteenth centuries, and its unknown builder would have had no shortage of such raw materials in the port.

Duke Street was one of the first thoroughfares where a new breed of wealthy entrepreneur, the rising middle-class gentry of the town, had begun to 'live over the shop'. It was here that they set up residences for themselves and their families in stylish

The Monro stands on Duke Street, which was named after the Duke of Cumberland in the mid-eighteenth century.

terraced properties. Many of these stood above or alongside the private warehouses, counting houses, stables, and carriage houses of each gentleman merchant. This was a time before the concept of separating business and private life had begun to evolve. It was also a time before the development of separate dockside warehouses for the storage of goods, and the building of banks with strong safes that could securely stockpile a merchant's accumulating wealth. Despite the depredations of time, Hitler, and a demolition-happy city council in the 1960s, a number of these multi-use buildings survive in and around Duke Street.

This street had also been laid out to directly connect the docks of Sailor Town with the mostly rural farmland and open heathland that then covered the fringes of the still relatively small town of Liverpool. It also enabled the gentry to begin moving into the squares and terraces of new 'out of town' homes, then being built in what is now known as Liverpool's Georgian Quarter, in the broad streets around the Anglican cathedral.

The creators of the graceful and tastefully decorated gastro-pub that is the modern Monro have preserved and restored much of the original town house, although the carriage house and stables have long since vanished. So too have the private storage and banking facilities, unless, of course, these were located in the large cellars and network of tunnels that still exist beneath the building. Some of these passages still lead down to what would have been the Old Dock, and which provided direct access to the ships that brought raw materials and commodities in and out of the port. Sadly, modern health and safety rules mean that these are currently inaccessible to the public.

The building, which is now Grade II listed, seems to have been first licensed as a public house from 1898, and there is a list of its licensees from that year until 1927 attractively displayed on a painted board mounted on the outside of the pub. Whether it too was previously a beer house is uncertain, unless its earlier merchant owners fell on hard times and needed to diversify.

Despite its eccentric spelling, The Monro is named after *The James Monroe*, which was a three-masted, square-rigged sailing ship, built in 1815 in America for the Black Ball Line. The letter 'e' is missing from the pub's name to distinguish it from another pub in the city, owned by the same people, which is confusingly named The James Monroe.

The Black Ball Line was founded in New York by a group of merchant Quakers, and they began with four packet ships: the *Amity*, *Courier*, *Pacific* and the *James Monroe*. Such vessels were originally smaller ships that made regular, scheduled sailings, initially carrying mail or cargo with only limited accommodation for passengers. They usually sailed only in local waters around the coasts of America, England and European countries. The ships were called 'packets' because they carried parcels, or separate consignments of goods, or groups of people.

However, in 1818 the *James Monroe* began the first scheduled, regular crossings between Liverpool and New York. The ship and the Black Ball Line not only entered the history books but also nautical folklore because of these pioneering voyages. In fact, the line is mentioned in several sea shanties, including 'Homeward Bound' and the more well-known 'Blow the Man Down'. The shipping line also had a dedicated sea shanty, 'Hurrah for the Black Ball Line'.

The *James Monroe* was named in tribute to the recently inaugurated and fifth American President (1758–1831), who was in office from 1817 to 1825. The ship set off from New York on 5 January 1818, and arrived in Liverpool on 2 February, which was an impressive speed for the time, and for the season. She carried eight passengers and a cargo of apples, flour, cotton, cranberries, hops, and wool. Before long, many other shipping lines copied the Black Ball Line. Now, vessels of all sizes, and with many cargoes of goods and people, soon began operating between Liverpool and America. Unfortunately, the *James Monroe* ran aground and foundered off the Tasmanian coast in 1850.

The Monro serves a wide range of excellent beers, wines, and spirits, to accompany an excellent menu, and wherever customers sit in the pub they find themselves in stylish surroundings. This is particularly true of the small but very comfortable private function rooms, which are upstairs. Here, it easy to imagine that you are actually in the elegant drawing rooms of an eighteenth-century gentleman and his family. When downstairs, though, customers need to be aware of the invisible ghost, which can certainly make its presence felt by moving around their glasses!

One of the delightful function rooms on the first floor.

The main bar. Note the bench seats and tables on the right – this is where the ghost most often manifests itself!

ALMA DE CUBA, St Peter's Church, Seel Street, Liverpool, L1 4BH

Sailor Town was so awash with taverns and places of other, more questionable, entertainments that Christians felt they had an important role to play in this community, especially among its seafarers. The final pub in this section is Alma de Cuba in Seel Street and, while many pubs in Liverpool are in interesting buildings, this is the only one inside a former Roman Catholic church.

Originally built in 1788 by Revd A. B. MacDonald (1736–1814), who was a Benedictine priest, the former church of St Peter stood alone in a field in largely rural surroundings. However, this was a period of great political instability in Britain, caused by the national fear of a rise in Catholic power. Britain was then a staunchly Protestant country, although one with a still large Catholic population. The unrest had come to a head during the Jacobite Rebellion of 1745. This was when the exiled Stuart family, in the person of the Catholic pretender to the English Crown, Bonnie Prince Charlie (1720–88), invaded England from Scotland in an attempt to regain the throne for his dynasty. Indeed, so fearful of an attack were the people of Liverpool that they fortified their town, but the rebels never arrived.

After the final routing of the Jacobites, attitudes to the Catholics began to relax somewhat; this was why Father MacDonald felt able to build his new church in Seel Street. In 1818, St Peter's was considerably enlarged as its congregation grew, mostly with overseas sailors from Roman Catholic countries. Following the emancipation of the Catholics, however, its worshippers now included many ordinary Catholic families, and it continued to serve the local community for 188 years. This was despite it being damaged a number of times during the May Blitz of 1941. On one occasion the roof was set on fire, and the building was miraculously saved although, a few years before this, another miracle had already saved the old church from fire.

A story tells how, during the time of Father Basil Primavessi as parish priest between 1929 and 1937, a fire broke out in the neighbourhood. The wind was blowing the flames towards the church so anxious parishioners roused the priest from his sleep. The Father simply made his way into the church, where he placed a medallion of St Benedict on the wall, and then returned to his bed. Father Basil's faith paid off, because the wind then changed direction and St Peter's was saved.

Because of a dwindling congregation, in 1976, what was by then the oldest surviving Catholic church in Liverpool, and one of the city's oldest buildings, St Peter's was forced to close. It was handed over to the local Polish Catholic community but, in 1978, it closed for good as a church. The building remained shut up and increasingly deteriorating, and was deconsecrated in 1993. It was then at serious risk of being demolished but was saved by the local development company, Urban Splash.

Following a major restoration and tasteful redesigning, Alma de Cuba opened as a bar and restaurant in 2005. It was created to focus on the food and culture of Cuba, hence its name, which is Spanish for 'Soul of Cuba'. Awarded 'Best Bar', 'Best Restaurant', and 'UKs Best Venue' in 2008 and 2009, Alma de Cuba still wins many accolades.

As the building was already Grade II listed, many of the original church fixtures and fittings remain in place, including the stained-glass panels. However, the large painting

Above: The old galleries of the church are now the ultra-modern dining area, overlooking the former nave and altar.

Below: The former nave of the old church is now the main bar area.

of St Peter that had previously hung behind the altar was removed to the Liverpool Metropolitan cathedral of Christ the King. A stunning mirror now replaces this. During the renovations, the bodies of eight monks and twenty-two lay people were found in the crypt. These were carefully disinterred and have been reburied elsewhere.

What was previously the nave of St Peter's remains an open space, but now with a long bar running its entire length up to the chancel steps, which still survive. In fact, this now forms the stage area, from which live music is performed by some of Liverpool's most talented singers and musicians. Above the nave, suspended from the ceiling, are three very large chandeliers. These are particularly unusual, though, as they are entirely made from sets of antlers!

The former lady chapel, on the right of the altar area, is now a large snug, beautifully decorated with a variety of old memorials and sculptural pieces. Its three original stained-glass windows add a special ambience to the room. The columns and portico surrounding what was the altar of St Peter's have all been carefully restored to their original colours and condition. This area of the building, together with the central space and bar area, are overlooked from the former galleries of the church, which now serve as the restaurant.

For one of the most unusual drinking and dining experiences in the city, and in historically very important surroundings, Alma de Cuba ranks among the very best in Liverpool.

Chapter Four

The Good-Time Girls

The area in and around Lime Street remains what it has been for over 150 years, a place of straightforward entertainment; however, this is now of a more savoury kind than was the case in earlier generations!

The land, upon which the next small selection of pubs now stands, was still largely open fields even in the opening decades of the nineteenth century. It was here that cockfighting, dogfighting, and bare-knuckle boxing were once favourite pastimes for local townsfolk, as was, as we shall see, indulging in the pleasures of the flesh!

MA EGERTON'S STAGE DOOR, 9 Pudsey Street, Liverpool, L1 1JA

Unlike Ma Boyle, Ma Egerton was very much a real person. Mary Egerton was the famous landlady of a number of Liverpool pubs, but was also well known in the international performing and entertainment community as a theatrical agent. Certainly a 'good-time girl', but only in the sense that she enjoyed life to the full, Mary wanted to ensure that others did too, especially her friends and the customers of her pubs.

Born in Ireland in 1863, not only does Mary have a fascinating history, but so does the gloriously theatrical pub that bears her name. What is now known as 'Ma Egerton's Stage Door' stands on the corner of Pudsey Street and Lord Nelson Street, directly opposite the Stage Door of Liverpool's famous Empire Theatre. While the origins of Lord Nelson Street are obvious, the other street is named after Pudsey Dawson (1752–1816). He was Mayor of Liverpool in 1799, but is more significant for being a major benefactor of Britain's first school for the blind. From 1800, this stood facing on to London Road, and covered all the land between the street that bears his name and Hotham Street, until it moved to new premises on Myrtle Street in 1850.

The land was then cleared when a glass and joinery merchant store, and large stables were built on the site, together with some houses. One of these was destined to become the pub, standing at No. 9 Pudsey Street. In 1864, this was listed as 'Hoffman's Coffee Shop' but, in 1869, the building seems to have been completely rebuilt. This was in an area now being described as 'very down at heel, and rife with arguments and rows from sailors and prostitutes extending along Lime Street, into Lord Nelson Street and along Pudsey Street'.

Right: Ma Egerton's Stage Door at
night; its most appropriate setting as
it stands so close to the stage door of
The Empire Theatre.

Below: The lounge.

Hoffman's Coffee Shop on the corner of Pudsey Street in 1864.

In all likelihood previously operating as another beer house, by 1878, the building had been licensed as a public house and named The Eagle. By 1891, the pub was standing next to a large tram and omnibus depot, with even larger stables. This was replaced in 1897 by a roller-skating rink and, in 1930, by a 4,000-seat boxing stadium. The Paramount Cinema, later The Odeon, then stood on the site, which is now home to new blocks of student apartments.

All of this activity continued to keep The Eagle busy with happy drinkers, as well as being a focal point for the good-time girls, who still actively serviced the neighbourhood in and around Lime Street. Indeed, this thoroughfare had already passed into international legend as the beat of prostitutes and other denizens of Liverpool's underworld.

Around 1890, Mary Egerton had come to Liverpool from Dublin, and had taken over as the landlady of The American Bar on nearby Lime Street. Because of her role as an international theatrical agent, she already numbered Charlie Chaplin and music hall singer Marie Lloyd among her many theatrical friends. Fred Astaire and his sister, Adele, were also friends of Mary Egerton, and shared convivial libations with her while appearing in Liverpool in 1928.

However, Mary mixed with people from all walks of life, which was essential as a Liverpool pub landlady. Indeed, one of her frequent statements was, 'Peer or pauper they're all the same to me'. She was also so respected in the theatre that, by acclaim, she was welcomed into the entertainers' charitable organisation, The Water Rats. She was its first non-performing member, and was awarded the special title of 'Lady Ratling'.

Ma Egerton either entertaining, or being entertained by, some young sailors in the 1940s.

Mary also played a crucial part in the capture of one of Britain's most notorious murderers, Hawley Harvey Crippen (*b.* 1862). He was married to the music hall singer, and friend of Mary, Cora Crippen (1873–1910), who used the stage name of Belle Elmore. On one of her many trips to London from Liverpool, early in 1910, Mary saw Crippen with an attractive young woman on his arm. Mary noticed that the girl, Ethel le Neve (1883–1967), was wearing a distinctive starburst brooch, which she recognised as belonging to her friend. As Belle had, by this time, been missing for some time, Mary reported her suspicions to the police. In due course Crippen was caught, tried, and found guilty of murdering and dismembering his wife. He was hanged in November 1910, largely thanks to Mary Egerton.

By 1930, Mary, now affectionately but respectfully known as 'Ma', had become the licensee of a number of pubs in Liverpool, including The Eagle, which became her flagship establishment. It was soon after this that the pub became popularly known as 'Ma Egerton's' in honour of its famous landlady. However, it would not be until 1980 that this would become the official name of the pub. In 1934, The Eagle was given a major interior refit by its brewery owners. The new oak panelling and bar that were then installed are still in existence today, helping to add to the style and theatrical flavour of the modern pub.

In the 1950s, The Eagle was taken over by Ma Egerton's daughter, Mamie, who continued to run it for another twenty years. During this time it remained a popular venue for performers appearing at Liverpool's theatres and clubs, including Judy Garland, Laurel and Hardy, Sammy Davis Jnr, Tom Jones, The Rolling Stones and, of course, The Beatles. In fact, in 1953, Frank Sinatra had to be called back to The Empire

Theatre from 'Ma E's' to complete the second half of one of his concerts. Resisting, he said that Ma's pub 'has the best Guinness I've ever tasted'.

In September 2012, the pub was bought by local actor and entrepreneur, Iain Hoskins, who spent £250,000 refurbishing the old building. This included its complete restoration and redecoration, while retaining all the original features of the pub. He also ensured that photographs of Ma Egerton, who died in the 1960s, and her celebrity customers lined its walls. Iain reopened the building in November 2012, now renamed as 'Ma Egerton's Stage Door'. In keeping with its traditions, and no doubt to the satisfaction of the shade of Mary Egerton, the official re-opening of the pub was a star-studded night of theatricality and celebration.

THE CROWN, 43 Lime Street, Liverpool, L1 1JQ

There has been a licensed pub at the corner of Skelhorne Street and Lime Street since 1859, probably already called The Crown. In 1905, the existing building was bought by Walkers Brewery, who completely rebuilt it. This was deliberately to compete with wealthy brewer Robert Cain, who was then remodelling 'gin palaces' all over Liverpool. To redesign their new pub, Walkers employed one of Cain's favourite architects, Liverpool-based Walter William Thomas (1849–1912). He did so in grand Art Nouveau and Fin de Siècle style, to produce the dramatic building, now Grade II* listed, which graces one of Liverpool's most famous and notorious streets.

The design and decoration of the pub's exterior is striking, and the elaborate lettering of the signs on its walls puts one in mind of the stylings of the Paris Metro. Even the doorways into The Crown invite you in to what you believe will be, and indeed proves to be, a palace. Inside, the large, airy, and well-lit public bar is indeed a fantasy of wood panelling, patterned tiling, polished brass work, beaten copper, etched glass, and extremely detailed moulded plasterwork, elements of which are picked out in gold leaf. This plasterwork deserves particular study, though, because of the several phallic objects that protrude from it, in various places.

These were left by the original plasterer, who was a cigar smoker. However, he never finished his cigars and had a habit of stubbing them out, while still quite lengthy, in whatever part of the plaster he was working on at the time! Then he coated them in plaster and left them as part of his creation. Some people say that, in fact, the craftsman actually left his stubs here because he had not been paid for the job. There are seven cigars to find, and bar staff happily challenge customers to see if they can locate them all.

The smaller rear lounge is just as fully and beautifully decorated as the pub's main room. The polished wood panelling is just as impressive; the plaster ceiling just as ornate (though without cigar stubs); and the etched-glass windows just as elegant. The room's fireplace is particularly attractive, with a wood surround and beaten copper hood, and a large mirror above the mantle. Near the entrance to the rear lounge, a graceful staircase winds its way up to the restaurant on the first floor, which was originally the billiard room. This passes beneath a large, impressive stained-glass dome, and from the restaurant there are excellent views of St George's Hall, Lime Street station, and Liverpool's Cultural Quarter.

Above: The main bar.

Right: Staff at The Crown: manager Stewart Hemus, with barmaids Marie Burns and Joyce McLinden.

By the end of the nineteenth century, Lime Street itself was already world famous, or perhaps infamous, as a place of prostitution and debauchery. In those days certain good-time girls were themselves already renowned, such as Mary Ellen, the Battleship, Jumping Jenny, the Horse, Tich Maguire, and Cast-Iron Kitty. They serviced sailors and other clients up and down the street and in and out of its inns, taverns, and rooming houses.

Of course, one of Liverpool's most famous working girls had already passed into legend by the time the new Crown was built. She was Maggie May – yes, she did exist, and lived in rooms in Duke Street sometime around the beginning of the nineteenth century. Maggie certainly was known for robbing the sailors she took into her bed, and a famous song tells her story.

The ballad of Maggie May has been sung in pubs, on street corners, at gatherings, and at ceilidhs all over Liverpool and beyond for around 150 years, but it began as a sea-shanty. Liverpool, as a seafaring town, is the source of hundreds of such ditties and fo'c'sle songs. Indeed, there is a reference to it in the diary of one, Charles Picknell, a sailor on the convict ship *Kains*, which sailed to Van Diemens Land (Tasmania) in the 1830s.

While the song says that Maggie was a thief who took advantage of the matelots who crossed her mattress, this was not generally true of Liverpool prostitutes. Indeed, especially during the late nineteenth and early decades of the twentieth centuries, when poverty, neglect, and disease were rife in the town, most of these women were simply impoverished girls, resorting to the only commodity they had left to sell to feed themselves, and often their children too.

That prostitution was rife in the Liverpool of those days is undeniable, just as it was in every other sea-port and major city across Britain and the world. But what of Maggie? Well, the song says it all:

> Oh Maggie Maggie May, they've taken her away,
> And she'll never walk down Lime Street anymore.
> For she's robbed so many sailors,
> And Captains of the Whalers;
> That dirty, robbing, no good, Maggie May.

The manager of The Crown, Stewart Hemus, who is clearly and justifiably proud of his pub, describes it as 'a grand old lady', and it certainly has a style and stateliness that sets it apart from so many other pubs in the country. Of course, some of the other 'grand old ladies', those good-time girls who drank in The Crown and traded out of it, just like Maggie May, 'will never walk down Lime Street anymore'!

THE VINES, 81 Lime Street, Liverpool, L1 1JQ

Opening in 1907, The Vines, like The Crown, was designed by Walter William Thomas but this time for the Robert Cain Brewery. Thomas was always very smartly dressed, in suit and spats. However, this was not the first pub to stand on the corner of Lime Street and Copperas Hill.

In 1813, Richmond's Snuggery opened on the site as a tavern. This was popular with sailors, local drovers, and with the 'working girls' of the district. In fact, tunnels still run from the cellar of the modern pub, down towards the river. These are said to have once supplied the Snuggery with contraband rum and tobacco. Even so, the tavern had a good reputation for 'the high quality of the ales and victuals'. Then, in 1867, the Snuggery was taken over by Mr A. B. Vines, after whom the present pub is named; contrary to popular opinion, the name never had anything to do with grapes or vineyards.

Business for Mr Vines was so good that, by 1888, he had extended his premises to include five adjacent buildings, then making what had become known as 'Vines's Tavern' one of the largest premises in the town. When Cain's acquired The Vines they immediately demolished the building. Thomas then replaced it with the magnificent combination of Edwardian Baroque and mock Scottish castle that we now have, which gained the pub its nickname of 'The Big House'. Thomas's somewhat eccentric design also included the construction of an entirely useless tower on the roof, which contains nothing but a very tiny room! However, the rest of his design was in keeping with his usual high standards, including the interior décor, which was carried out by Gustav Hiller and The Bromsgrove Guild.

The large bar of The Vines is entered through the main entrance from the street. Its polished wooden floors, original mahogany bar with its brass fittings, and the stained-glass screens, are certainly impressive, as is the complex moulded plasterwork on the ceilings. From here, through a glorious polished-oak archway surmounted by a clock, customers pass along an ornate but narrow passageway into the Lounge Bar. One of the most striking features here is the marble-fronted fireplace with its pair of wooden caryatids that support the beaten copper overmantle and mahogany surround. From here, and also beneath elaborate ceiling plasterwork, a large doorway leads into the smoke room.

The fireplace in this very comfortable space is a perfect example of the skills of Hiller and the Guild, with its Art Nouveau copper fireplace surround, and very detailed beaten copper panel of a fully-crewed Viking longboat. Above this is a large moulded plaster panel showing a group of children frolicking in an Arcadian setting. However, what is considered to be the most stunning room in The Vines is the grand lounge, standing at the rear of the building.

Here, below a large, glass dome in this huge space, is another wealth of wooden panelling. This is dominated by a huge, ornate fireplace and mirror, overlooking the polished-wood ballroom floor (although this was created as a billiard room). All of this sits beneath three great crystal chandeliers and yet another powerful plaster ceiling. The Vines is indeed a 'big house'.

For well over 100 years, many customers of The Vines have been guests staying at the grand hotel that stands across the road, which is the world-famous Adelphi. This opened in 1914, and replaced two previous hotels of the same name: the first built in 1826, and a second, built in 1876. The first Adelphi Hotel had replaced the entrance to the former Ranelagh Tea Gardens, which was one of three landscaped pleasure gardens that graced Liverpool during the eighteenth century.

Left: The Vines; the 'Big House'.

Below: The rear bar, with its remarkable carved woodwork and fine brass.

The present hotel was once one of the most luxurious hotels in Britain. It serviced rail and ocean-going liner passengers and accommodated them in opulent surroundings. Nevertheless, The Vines, and Lime Street, of course, held such renowned and notorious attractions that many of the hotel's well-heeled gentlemen guests wanted to experience these interesting entertainments for themselves.

Many of the greatest performers who appeared in Liverpool, and who drank in The Vines as well as in Ma Egerton's, always stayed in The Adelphi. These included Mae West, Bing Crosby, Charlton Heston, Dame Margot Fontaine, and Rudolph Nureyev. VIP guests have also included many crowned heads of Europe and the world, as well as US President Franklin Roosevelt (1882–1945) and his wife, Eleanor, and Sir Winston Churchill. However, whether or not they too got to know any of Liverpool's good-time girls this story does not tell!

On 20 November 1956, customers of The Vines joined the thousands of people who filled Ranelagh Place, in front of The Adelphi. This was for the much-anticipated unveiling of a new colossal statue. This had been commissioned by Lewis's for the front of their newly rebuilt department store, standing across from the pub. During the May Blitz, the large store had been destroyed by Nazi high-explosive and incendiary bombs. The new store had reopened in 1951, and it was now time for the finishing touch because the renowned, if eccentric, sculptor, Jacob Epstein (1880–1959), was about to reveal his work.

The work of art that is the snug fireplace.

This had taken him 2 1/2 years to complete, and it had been hoisted into place under massive tarpaulins to preserve the mystery. As the covering fell away a great cheer went up, but this immediately changed to great shouts. Some of these were of shock, some of outrage, but mostly of amused delight. This was because, now dominating the store as well as one of Liverpool's busiest crossroads, was the very much larger-than-life-size, blatantly full-frontal, bronze figure of a completely naked man.

He still stands there today, with a determined expression and stance, on the prow of a great ship that seems to be surging out of the front of the building. He is piloting the vessel forward and going boldly into the future, which is why he is officially named 'Liverpool Resurgent'. However, he quickly became known by the more appropriate nickname of 'Dickie Lewis'! The ship's prow weighs 2 1/2 tons, and the figure itself weighs a further 2 3/4 tons. He stands at 18 feet and 6 inches tall overall, but I have no information about any other dimensions associated with the figure!

The great nude man became the topic of debate and discussion for many weeks after this – in the newspapers, at bus stops, in offices and factories, in front rooms, and in the bars of pubs just like The Vines.

The massive grand lounge, which was originally created as a billiard room!

Chapter Five

A Street Called 'Hope'

The last chapter in this book centres on Hope Street, which connects Liverpool's two great cathedrals. These are the Roman Catholic Metropolitan Cathedral of Christ the King, consecrated in 1967, and the Anglican Cathedral of Christ, begun in 1904, and completed in 1978. However, the street is actually named after William Hope, a local merchant and farmer, who built the first house in the street on the site of the present Philharmonic Hotel and Dining Rooms.

For those readers with an astrological or pagan bent, it is said that a ley-line runs the length of Hope Street. Allegedly, ley lines, or leys, are straight lines of strong spiritual energy, which align ancient worship sites or holy places. These may cover distances of anything from 1 or 2, to 9 or 10 miles. Many people believe that this is the reason why the builders and planners of both cathedrals were drawn to this location in the city. This is also said to be why the area has such a particular creative energy and cultural vibrancy.

Whatever the reason may be, Hope Street is certainly a centre of faith and hope, but especially of human expression, particularly in the arts, music, dance, and drama. It is also a neighbourhood of individuality, passion, and community, which is reflected in my final selection of Liverpool city's most historic and significant pubs.

PETER KAVANAGH'S, 2–6 Egerton Street, Liverpool, L8 7LY

This pub represents the tastes, energy, and prejudices of one man – Peter Kavanagh. He was very much a man of his time, which was the turn of the nineteenth and twentieth centuries.

The pub that bears the name of its well-known landlord stands at the end of a terrace of late-eighteenth-century private houses, at No. 2 Egerton Street. Previously yet another beer house, it was licensed in 1849 as a public house named The Liver Hotel. However, it retained the three-room layout of the original Georgian house. Then, in 1897, the pub was completely refurbished and renamed The Grapes, and Peter Kavanagh became its licensee.

The main bar in Peter Kavanagh's; cluttered but definitely cosy.

Although Kavanagh's birthdate is not clear, it is known that he was an Irish immigrant who had come to Liverpool as a child with his family, probably in the later 1800s. Despite his humble beginnings, Kavanagh became a capable and astute businessman. This meant that The Grapes quickly became very popular and successful, but Peter Kavanagh was also ambitious.

He had a passion for the romantic history of old sailing ships so, in 1911, he drew up plans for the complete redesigning all of the pub interiors to reflect the cabins of old galleons. However, due to the outbreak of the First World War, this had to be delayed. Fortuitously, the wait was worth it because, in 1927, the new Rialto Music and Dance Hall opened. Previously standing nearby in Upper Parliament Street, but sadly destroyed in the Toxteth Riots of 1981, this very popular dance hall did not serve alcohol. This meant that its customers were now spending their money in The Grapes regularly, and in their hundreds.

By 1929, Kavanagh had so much money that he could not only fulfil his plans for his pub, he could afford to buy it, which he did, from Liverpool Corporation on a ninety-nine-year lease. This included his purchase of No. 4 Egerton Street, which he then knocked through to double the size of his premises. Kavanagh now proceeded to

Peter Kavanagh's.

completely rebuild The Grapes, inside and out, and he certainly put the stamp of his personality on his pub.

Wood-panelled throughout, with two delightful snugs, a long corridor bar, and a very large lounge in three sections, today the pub has age and tradition embedded into its fabric. The eccentricity of its decoration only adds to its very distinctive character, reflecting that of Kavanagh himself. He commissioned a series of hand-carved wooden gargoyles, to decorate new picture rails that he installed throughout the pub, all made of oak. These were the work of some of the master craftsmen then building Liverpool's nearby Anglican Cathedral, and they are caricatures of some of Kavanagh's customers at that time. The ends of the bench armrests in the snugs are all of Kavanagh himself, so he certainly had a sense of humour.

In the front snug are colourful stained-glass windows that were created by craftsman William English, who also installed large stained-glass windows in Worcester Cathedral. As Kavanagh had a passion for all things nautical, in these are shown images of a lighthouse, a fully-rigged sailing ship, and crossed oars. English also designed the windows in the rear snug, in which are shown images of an eighteenth-century stagecoach, the coats of arms of Oxford and Cambridge Universities and Robert Stephenson's famous steam locomotive, the *Rocket*.

Perhaps what is most impressive about the decoration of the pub, though, are original murals, painted on the curved walls of each snug. Created also in 1929, these are the work

The reason why the 'Hogarth Room' has a different modern name!

of Scottish artist Eric Robinson. In the front snug is a scene, 11 feet long, from Charles Dickens' very popular novel, *The Posthumous Papers of the Pickwick Club*. This is why the snug is known as the 'Pickwick Room'. The characters shown are also caricatures of many of Kavanagh's customers, and the landlord himself is portrayed as the very thin and ungainly man, wearing a tall hat, standing directly behind Mister Pickwick.

The mural in the rear snug is 13 feet long, and is made up of several scenes in the style of Hogarth. These include the Gin Lady, presiding over scenes of happy excess in the streets and taverns of London. This is why this is known as the 'Hogarth Room'. During Kavanagh's time, this room was reserved for only his most elite clientele and for his personal friends. It is therefore certain that he would not approve of the collection of objects that now hang down from the ceiling of this snug, which have given it its other name of the 'Piss-Pot Room'!

In fact, the walls and the ceilings of the entire pub are now ornamented with the most curious collection of objets d'art, ephemera, memorabilia, and oddities. These can all provide stimulating conversation pieces if ever dialogue between drinkers dries up. However, well lubricated by the fine beers served here, this would be extremely unlikely in this cultural, artistic, and political hotbed.

Always conscious of his personal social standing, and of the status of his pub, until the end of the Second World War Kavanagh was very strict about the type of people he allowed on his premises. This became a social gathering place for only the upper

The Hogarth Room's stained-glass windows.

echelons of local society, including magistrates, senior police officers and public officials, merchants and businessmen, and gentlemen of only the most impeccable credentials.

Because of his very fixed views, you could also only drink in his pub if you were male and white, otherwise you would not be allowed to cross his threshold. Women were only allowed in if accompanied by gentlemen, and could only sit quietly in the rear snug because he believed they made his pub look untidy. If they were found to be standing or walking around then he had them immediately ejected, no matter who they were with!

Peter Kavanagh was also a successful entrepreneur and designer, who patented many inventions, including flip-up theatre and cinema seats. He married a local girl, is believed to have had three sons and two daughters, and was licensee of The Grapes until his death in 1950. One of his sons then took over the license but the business began to fail. In 1977, the family sold the pub to a brewery, who then extended it into No. 6 Egerton Street. Still known as The Grapes, the pub was only renamed in honour of its illustrious landlord in 1978, but it now thrives as a very popular centre of local social and cultural life.

THE BELVEDERE HOTEL, 5 Sugnall Street, Liverpool, L7 7EB

The 'small but perfectly formed' Belvedere Hotel stands in Sugnall Street, off Falkner Street, and the entire block of houses has Grade II listed status. The pub was built on the site of an eighteenth-century tea rooms, which had been converted from an old hayloft. In those days, this entire area was largely rural and regarded as being out in the country.

As we have seen, this was a time when the gentry of the town were moving into the district to live. Now, the townspeople of Liverpool too were making their way up Duke Street, from the congested, dirty, and undoubtedly smelly town, on outings to enjoy the fresh air and open spaces. The tea rooms serviced visitors to a large pleasure gardens that then stood near here, known as 'The Spring Tea Gardens'. The Belvedere, meaning 'beautiful view', would take its name from this attractive, open, and cultivated landscape.

On land now covered by blocks of student apartments, members of gentile Georgian and early Victorian society would meet at the Spring Tea Gardens. Among topiary hedges, landscaped gardens and flower beds, strolling past fish ponds and wooded bowers, they would listen to music played by string quartets wafting around them on the summer breezes. Beautiful and graceful ladies in their finest gowns, with their hooped skirts, would seem to glide along the pathways. Their bonnets framed pale faces, and their delicate lace shawls kept out the chill of the evening air. They would promenade along on the arms of their beaus, each gentleman immaculately turned out in their buckled shoes, and in neatly tailored suits with their double-breasted fronts, large buttons, and flawless silk cravats.

What is now The Belvedere was originally a private house belonging to a master mariner, which was erected in 1836. Then, in 1848, the property became a beer house and auction room. Ale was sold across the threshold from what remains a tiny front

Belvedere landlord, John O'Dowd, savouring a glass of his own Liverpool Gin.

room and lobby but, because of its limited size, it is unlikely that auction sales were ever carried out here. It is more probable that this was the administrative offices of the auction house, which traded in ships' cargoes.

No. 8 Sugnall Street had become The Belvedere Hotel by the later decades of the nineteenth century, when it was first refurbished and reopened as such by the Bents Brewery. However, it never actually provided accommodation – it was just that putting the word 'hotel' after your pub's name gave it greater status. The pub then passed into the ownership of Bass Charrington, then Thwaites, and then into private ownership, which is still the case today.

Fortunately, the Victorian architecture and design of The Belvedere remain largely unaltered, and the public bar in particular is an eccentric delight. The curved, highly-polished wooden bar, with its tall stools, gives the tiny space a comfortable intimacy. At the far end of this is a door, which is now an office, but which once led to an off-licence. Customers, often children sent by their parents when licensing laws were less stringently observed, would come to a side entrance in what is now the alley alongside the pub. Here, their empty jugs would be filled with beer to be taken back home.

The bar, once directly opening on to the street, is now accessed from a short, narrow lobby leading from the front door. This also doubles as a very compact snug, and is separated from the bar by an original and ornate screen. In wooden frames, this partition comprises four, intricately etched, sliding glass serving hatches, and this feature of the pub is quite rare in the north-west of England.

The 'small but perfectly formed' Belvedere.

On the left of the lobby is the small smoke room, and the pub is tastefully decorated throughout, and adorned with pictures and photographs, a number with connections to John Lennon. He drank here, as well as in The Grapes and a number of other pubs throughout the city. One of these pictures is a copy of a sketch of John as a young man, drawn in 1958, by Helen Anderson. She was a fellow student with John at the nearby Art College in Hope Street.

Behind the bar is an amazing array of bottled spirits, mostly varieties of gin, which betray the main passion of The Belvedere's enthusiastic licensee, John O'Dowd. Apart from the sale of fine, local, cask-conditioned craft ales, he is driving forward the distilling, bottling, and sale of his own 'Liverpool Gin'. Taking over the licence of The Belvedere in 2009, in 2012 John became aware of the rise in popularity of micro-breweries and micro distilleries, and he saw a gap in the market in Liverpool. Only too happy to regale his customers with his knowledge of the history of the brewing and distilling industry in Britain, John will also wax lyrical about his product and his tasting school, which he has named the 'GinNasium'!

John is proud of his new gin, and his pub, stating that, 'You can't be average anymore, you have to be the very best!' This means that a pub that once served ales and spirits to the gentry of Victorian Liverpool is now continuing to do so to a new generation of discerning drinkers with sophisticated palates, still in a district that is the heart of the cultural and artistic community of the modern city.

The Belvedere's extraordinary tasting 'GinNasium'.

The smoke room in The Belvedere.

YE CRACKE, 13 Rice Street, Liverpool, L1 9BB,

Despite its seemingly 'Olde English' name, the pub is actually no older than 1852, when it first opened as The Ruthin Castle. Prior to this it had probably been a beer house, standing in a terrace of small cottages, which backed on to an old court dwelling. These were blocks of often sordid, squalid, and overcrowded rooms, built on three or four sides of a central courtyard, and frequently on a number of levels.

There may have been a water pump in the yard, but this was rare. There may also have been a privy, which would have been just as rare. This would actually have been far from private as they seldom had doors, and it would not have been connected to any sort of sewage system. This made the living conditions extremely unpleasant for those families unfortunate enough to be forced to reside in them.

Such court dwellings survived all over inner-city Liverpool, and some of its poorer suburbs, until just after the Second World War. A sign is still mounted on the side of the pub, pointing the way to 'Court Number 1'. The former courtyard is now the beer garden of Ye Cracke, with fortunately no remaining evidence of its previous use.

In 1862, the then landlord of the Ruthin Castle bought the cottage next door and extended his premises, which was then only nicknamed as 'Ye Cracke'. The reasons for this are now lost in the mists of time, although I speculate that as the passage alongside

The main bar, with the doorway through to the rear bar and the rest of this charming pub.

the pub was once the narrow entrance to the former court, this was called the 'crack'. I think that the 'Ye' was an affectation of the brewery, who appear to have taken it over and registered it as such in 1892.

The pub entrance opens onto a tiny, L-shaped bar, from which a narrow doorway then leads into the rest of the premises, which are surprisingly spacious. Indeed, Ye Cracke is made up of a fascinating collection of differently sized rooms, only one of which actually has listed status. This is a small snug off the back bar known as the 'War Office'. A glass panel above its doorway describes this as such. The tiny room gained its name from the fact that it was here that older drinkers, in the late nineteenth century, would discuss the progress of the Boer War (1899–1902) then taking place in South Africa. These gentlemen were banished to this room to prevent them boring the other customers in the pub.

In keeping with the fact that this pub lies just off the supposed ley line along Hope Street, Ye Cracke has been at the heart of the artistic and musical subcultures of the city for generations. In fact, from the late nineteenth century it was described as a 'musical snuggery', where groups of close-harmony male singers, known as 'Glee Clubs', would meet to practice. This tradition continues today, with frequently ad-hoc performances by musicians and singers of varying levels of ability, inevitably leading to rousing choruses from all those assembled in the pub.

Ye Cracke, with the side passage that once led to 'Court No 1'.

I have very happy memories of Ye Cracke in the 1960s when, as a young man aged eighteen or so, I regularly spent Friday nights here with my mates. We would sing along to the songs of Bob Dylan and others, accompanied by anyone who could play an acoustic guitar. We would swig vast quantities of Newcastle Brown Ale straight out of the bottles before doing so became fashionable, and bang out the rhythm of the music on the large, wooden tables – halcyon days!

Indeed, it was from the early 1960s, and the heyday of the Merseybeat era, that the pub took on a new significance. As well as drinking in The Grapes in Mathew Street, and in The Belvedere, it was here that John Lennon would often skive off from his studies at the art college, where he met his future wife, Cynthia Powell (*b.* 1939), at a college dance. Afterwards, he took her to Ye Cracke for a drink, and then round to the flat of his best friend, Stuart Sutcliffe (1941–62). Cynthia often stayed here overnight with John after a few drinks in Ye Cracke, having told her mother that she was sleeping over with a girlfriend.

Ye Cracke was like a second home to John and Stuart, and it was a great tragedy when, on 10 April 1962, Stuart Sutcliffe (often referred to as 'the Fifth Beatle') died in Hamburg, of a cerebral haemorrhage, at the age of only twenty-one.

In the small bar of the pub hang a number of early photographs of John, Stuart, and Cynthia, some taken in and around Ye Cracke. Around the walls of the rest of

The beer garden that was once the old and squalid courtyard dwelling.

the pub hang paintings and art of all descriptions. Some is modern, and for sale, and some is much older, and definitely not available for purchase. These include an excellent collection of sketches and watercolours of Liverpool streets and buildings from the mid-1960s. In fact, along the full length of the main lounge hangs a gloriously complicated and colourful artist's impression of what the Battle of Waterloo looked like. It was in this part of the pub that John, Stuart, and the 'Dissenters' liked to drink.

The Dissenters was a group formed by John Lennon, but which never performed! It was made up of students from the art college, including Stuart, as well as Bill Harry (*b.* 1939), who actually coined of the term 'Merseybeat', and their friend, Rod Murray (*b.* 1937). A plaque on the wall of the rear bar describes how this group came about:

This plaque commemorates John Lennon's 'other band' which never played a note.

In June 1960, these 4 art students attended a poetry reading by Royston Ellis (the 'Paperback Writer' in Paul McCartney's song 1966); Ellis's work was heavily influenced by Allen Ginsberg and other Americans. Afterwards, the 4 came here to discuss what they'd heard. They were unimpressed and decided to put Liverpool 'on the map' each in their own way as 'The Dissenters'; the rest is…

Warm and welcoming Zardia Naif, the licensee of Ye Cracke.

Though undoubtedly another eccentric pub, the place has a genuine charm and appeal, and not just because of its historic associations. Fine ales and good company in informal surroundings are also what make Ye Cracke such a special place.

THE ROSCOE HEAD, 24 Roscoe Street, Liverpool, L1 2SX

The Roscoe Head is named in tribute to a man often described as 'Liverpool's Greatest Citizen', and it stands in a street also named after this remarkable character.

In 1753, William Roscoe was himself born the son of a publican in The Bowling Green Tavern, which once stood at the corner of Hope Street and Mount Pleasant, and he went on to have a very successful career. Training as a lawyer, and living in Liverpool all his life, Roscoe was also an historian, an art collector, and the founder of Liverpool's original botanic gardens.

He was an intellectual, a free thinker, a great social reformer, and a vociferous campaigner against slavery, which was then the principal source of great income for many of his leading fellow citizens. Indeed, one of his many written works, *The Wrongs of Africa*, helped fuel the abolitionist movement in Britain, and it encouraged his many friends and colleagues in Liverpool to join him in the campaign.

William Roscoe was eager to promote cultural development in his home town, fearing that this was being left behind by a drive to simply create wealth. He was active in the formation of the Liverpool Royal Institution in 1814, and of the Lyceum Club in 1802, and he became a significant collector of books and paintings. In fact, his paintings became the core of the current collection of Liverpool's Walker Art Gallery, and part of his library is now in the Liverpool Athenaeum Club, which he had already helped to establish in 1797.

The Roscoe Head.

This true 'Renaissance man' was also a banker and a merchant, a keen amateur scientist, and a poet. Indeed, his charming children's verses, 'The Butterfly Ball' and 'The Grasshopper's Feast', have never been out of print. He was known and respected not only in his home town but throughout Britain and abroad. Indeed, writing of his visit to Liverpool, the well-known American author, Washington Irving (1783–1859), who wrote among other things, *Tales from Sleepy Hollow* and *Rip Van Winkle*, said,

> One of the first places to which a stranger is taken in Liverpool is The Athenaeum …
> my attention was drawn to a person just entering the room … it was Roscoe. I drew
> back with an involuntary feeling of veneration. This then was an author of celebrity;
> this was one of those men whose voices have gone forth to the ends of the earth.

In 1806, William Roscoe became MP for Liverpool, speaking vociferously and regularly in Parliament for the abolition of slavery, and for parliamentary reform to extend the right to vote to a greater number of ordinary people. A radical who genuinely cared about the working man and the poor, and who fought against injustice, in 1807, Roscoe also campaigned for the emancipation of Roman Catholics, and for free education and schools for the working classes. In fact, although resented by the slave ship owners and regarded by others as a controversial militant, he was still held in such honour in the town that Roscoe Street was named after him in 1796. This was thirty-five years before his death, which took place in 1831.

A life-long Unitarian, William Roscoe was buried in Liverpool, in the grounds of the Renshaw Street Unitarian chapel. Although this has now become a bar and restaurant, the burial ground survives and has been renamed as the Roscoe Memorial Gardens.

A statue of Roscoe stands among other representations of Liverpool's Victorian great and good in St George's Hall, in the centre of the city's St George's Quarter.

The current landlady of The Roscoe Head, Carol Ross, is very proud of her small but delightful pub, and of the man that gave it its name. Consisting of a small bar and drinking lobby, entered directly from the narrow street, off which are two small rooms and a very compact snug, Carol and her regulars make every new visitor very welcome indeed. In fact, the pub is renowned for its hospitality and gentle conviviality.

The building itself was erected in the mid-eighteenth century as a private family home, and had a variety of occupants. However, by 1843, it was the home and workshop of Pellegrino Casciani (1780–1866). Born in Italy, he came to Liverpool, as did so many people, to seek his fortune. He was a skilled and popular modeller and figure maker in plaster of paris, and was very successful. He made and sold plaster busts of famous characters and leading figures of the day, as well as accepting commissions for portrait busts and death masks. This was very fashionable during the early decades of the nineteenth century.

By 1848, the building had become part of a post office, and in that year it was divided into smaller premises, one of which became a licensed public house listed as The Roscoe Head. A portrait of the head of William Roscoe, naturally, forms the pub's exterior sign.

Carol and her family have run the pub for more than thirty years, and she made a very particular point of telling me that, in the *Good Beer Guide*, The Roscoe Head is listed as one of its 'Magnificent 7'. This means that it is one of only seven pubs in Britain that have featured in every edition of the guide since it was first published in 1974.

Main bar.

Redesigned in the 1930s, and then refitted in 2006, the inside of the pub has no particular architectural or design merit, but neither has it been spoilt in any way. It is a charming and comfortable place to while away an hour or two, in good, Liverpudlian company, and where conversation and companionship reign supreme, in keeping with the personality and philosophy of William Roscoe.

THE PHILHARMONIC DINING ROOMS, 36 Hope Street, Liverpool, L1 9BX

The Phil, or to give it is correct name, The Philharmonic Dining Rooms, is genuinely stunning. Indeed, CAMRA describes it as being 'the most spectacular pub in England'. The building, with its solid but tastefully ornate Edwardian exterior stonework, was commissioned by Robert Cain. Like The Crown and The Vines, this was designed by Walter William Thomas and, once again, he threw himself into his commission.

As with the Vines, The Phil has the look of a Scots baronial hall but this time with Tudor overtones. In the stonework can be seen stepped gables and turrets, oriel windows, and a balustraded parapet. There are also relief sculptures of musicians and musical instruments. This is all in tribute to the Philharmonic Hall, which stands diagonally across from The Phil, on the opposite corner of Hope Street. The first internationally renowned classical concert hall was opened on the site in 1849, but this burnt down in 1933. It was replaced by the current and equally renowned building in 1939.

Listed as Grade II*, the pub was built between 1898 and 1900, and even its main entrance gates are dramatic. These are made in wrought iron and gilded copper, in a very elaborate Art-Nouveau style, and they carry the arms of the original Robert Cain brewery and the company motto. This reads as *Pacem Amo*, and translates as 'I Love Peace'. The gates were designed by Henry Bloomfield Bare (1848–1912), who was a Liverpool-based designer and President of the Liverpool Architectural Society.

The Phil's distinctive and impressive interior design work was principally carried out by the University of Liverpool School of Applied Art, and the pub is a main feature on all the guided tour trails. In fact, the pub was first built by Cain as a private gentlemen's club, for the elite of the city. This joined other, although much larger, institutions such as The Athenaeum, The Lyceum, and The Artists' Club. It remained a private establishment until around the late 1920s, when it then became a high-class public house.

The main drinking lobby, with its mosaic floor, semi-circular bar, and original columns and brass fittings, houses a large and splendid inglenook fireplace. This has a marble and wood surround and a large, circular mirror. It is flanked on each side by beaten copper panels bearing images of musicians. There are also stained-glass panels bearing images of Lord Baden-Powell and Field Marshall Earl Roberts. The lobby also adjoins two snugs, individually named Brahms and Liszt! This was not the idea of Robert Cain, but of a much later landlord sometime in the 1970s, who clearly had a wry sense of humour.

From the main bar a short and narrow corridor leads to the magnificently ornate, and very spacious, grand lounge. With its high ceiling, intricately moulded cornices and

The main bar, with the intricate ceiling and carved column. Notice the entrance to the snug named 'Liszt'.

plasterwork, panelled woodwork, and stained-glass windows, this is the most luxurious part of the building, yet it was originally built as a billiard room. The large fireplace, with its carved wooden surround and ornate plaster panel above the mantelpiece, dominates the room, as do the large carved figures of the god Pan, and numerous Dryads. These look down on the clientele from their positions above the high walls. This room also has beaten copper panels showing landscapes from around the Liverpool area. The rather small ladies' lavatories that lead off the lounge were only added sometime in the 1940s. Typically, as we have already seen, women were generally not allowed into pubs until well into the twentieth century, and never unaccompanied until the 1970s.

While the ladies' lavatories are both basic and plainly decorated, not so the gents' toilet – especially the urinals. These are luxurious indeed, and world famous in their

The Art Nouveau gates to the main entrance of The Phil.

own right. They are made from a particularly attractive 1890s 'Rouge Royale' roseate marble, and are a must-see (if not must-use) for any visitor. However, do check that they are unoccupied first, as it could prove problematic to be closely scrutinising the facilities, especially while they are in use, regardless of your gender!

Because of this risk, one woman tourist was too embarrassed to look at the urinals herself, even though assured that they were empty. She asked a couple of young men if they would be so kind as to take her camera and photograph these architectural wonders on her behalf. Like all Liverpudlians, they were very willing to oblige, and welcomed the opportunity to help a stranger. However, as these lads were indeed typical Scousers, their sense of humour took over. When the woman had her photos developed and printed, ready to show her friends and family, full frontal images of the urinals were not her only souvenir.

Another young man who used these urinals was a fledgling pop star from London, by the name of Stuart Leslie Goddard (*b.* 1954). As he was standing in the stall, with his future in his hands, he noticed its brand name, 'Adamant'. This inspired him to rename himself 'Adam Ant'! Goddard himself, however, does not like this story (I wonder why?), so he says he named himself after the insects, because 'they are resilient little buggers'.

The dining rooms on the first floor are also sumptuously decorated in carved wood, stained glass, and intricate mosaic work. At one point the pub was registered as The Philharmonic Hotel, although it has never provided public accommodation, but there have always been well-appointed dining facilities on the first floor. These are popular with modern-day diners and serve an extensive menu of traditional pub fare.

Many famous people have drunk in The Phil over the years, ranging from Yehudi Menuhin to Bob Dylan, and from Marc Bolan to Eric Clapton. Although, when asked what the downside of being famous was, John Lennon answered, 'Not being able to go for a pint in The Phil'!

If you visit The Philharmonic Dining Rooms you will always be in good company, famous or not, but certainly don't miss the urinals – in more senses than one!

THE CASA, 29 Hope Street, Liverpool, L1 9BQ

The building that is now the Casa, at No. 29 Hope Street, was built in the early nineteenth century as a large home for a single family, with rooms for servants on the attic floor. The building stands just across the road from The Philharmonic Dining Rooms, and yet the origins of that pub, and of the Casa Bistro and Bar, could not be more different.

Many public houses have often had just as much political and cultural relevance as they have had social significance, and they have certainly always been places of entertainment and relaxation. They have also always been, and continue to be, places of debate, argument, decision, campaign, and action – especially when the working classes have needed to find a voice.

I have deliberately chosen the Casa to be the last pub in this book because of why it was founded, and because of the socio-political role it still performs, especially among the working-class community of the city. The Casa is not simply a pub; the bar is only one part of 'The Initiative Factory'. This is a charitable trust that was established by sacked and redundant dockers, in the wake of an acrimonious strike on Liverpool docks, in the 1990s. Their aim was to use the building as an advice centre for themselves and for their fellow citizens.

Throughout the history of Liverpool, thousands of ships have come to the port from around the world. They brought with them foodstuffs, spices, tobacco, cotton, livestock, trade goods, fabrics, minerals, metals, and machinery. These were the raw materials that were driving forward the Industrial Revolution, as well as the expansion of Britain, her Empire, and her overseas interests, well into the twentieth century.

All these goods had to be moved and, despite the growth of mechanisation throughout the nineteenth and twentieth centuries, manpower remained the cheapest and most effective method of cargo handling. This is why the Liverpool dockers were so vital to the life of the port. Nevertheless, in the 1970s, the Mersey Docks and Harbour Board was hit by a financial crisis, almost being forced into bankruptcy and complete closure. The management of ports and docks across Britain had also failed to come to terms with the new working practices established after the Second World War, neither had they adapted to technical changes taking place in the maritime industry.

This instability was as obvious to the dockers and their trade unions as it was to the management, industrial relations broke down, and neither side was prepared to compromise. The unions called a national dockers' strike, which in due course was resolved, but only temporarily. While there was a period of relative calm at Liverpool Docks, in 1995, another dispute broke out at the port. The dockers went out on strike

Above: The Casa.

Left: The original
'Casablanca Club'
sign.

and, as a result, eighty men were sacked. They set up an unofficial picket line and, the next day, a further 329 men were sacked for refusing to cross this.

Replacement labour was then brought in by management, and these men were seen as strike-breakers and scabs by the striking dockers, and there were many outbreaks of violence. This strengthened the determination of the dockers not to give in, and the strike lasted until 1998, following an unprecedented 850 days. However, the ultimate victory of the employers was inevitable, as they were over-manned anyway, and so the sacked dockers had to acknowledge defeat. Because of their resolve, the Liverpool dockers now became national, working-class folk heroes. Even so, the role of dockers themselves, and of labour systems on the Liverpool docks, had changed forever.

As dedicated supporters of the dockers, film producer Ken Loach, and playwright and screenwriter Jimmy McGovern then began to work closely with the sacked and redundant men, and their families. Together, they produced the powerful Channel 4 television drama-documentary entitled *Dockers*. This was broadcast in 1999, and it told the human and political story of the Liverpool dock strike. The profits from this enabled The Initiative Factory to acquire No. 29 Hope Street from its then owners, Liverpool City Council, and to open it in December 2000.

The building then began its new life as a meeting place and support centre for the people of Liverpool, and to provide free welfare, housing, and employment advice. Founded on the belligerent independence and innate sense of justice and fairness which so characterise Scousers, the Casa takes its name from the 'Casablanca'. This was a legendary late-night Liverpool bar that once occupied the same building, run by the immigrant Somali community and largely serving sections of the local black population. The fan-light sign for the Casablanca now hangs inside the building.

The bar in the Casa had initially been set up simply to provide an income stream to maintain the building and to support the work of the charity, whose key objective remains, 'to alleviate poverty for the people of the City of Liverpool'. However, it has now established itself as a very popular pub in its own right.

While the bar and its adjoining lounge are the first things one sees upon walking up the steps into the building, at the rear of the ground floor is a large meeting room with a stage. Regular trade union and political meetings are held here. The room is also open for public use: for concerts and shows, and for dance classes, drama groups, and community meetings, as well as by faith groups ranging from Christians to pagans. This large extension was constructed by the dockers themselves, who also carried out all the initial restoration and redesign work of the entire building. The stairs from the bar lead to the upper floors, where the advice centre, training rooms, offices, and other facilities are situated.

For those people who simply want a good night out, but in surroundings that are far from frivolous, then the Casa is an excellent place to go. However, customers are made especially welcome if they also enjoy serious conversation about serious issues, and they will be in the company of trade unionists, political activists, journalists, students, and ordinary members of the community. The food is good, as is the range of beers that are available. The service is friendly, and the bar also has what it described as 'A Marxist Jukebox' – no one pays!

Acknowledgements

In this book it has only been the restrictions of space that have limited the number of stories that I have been able to pass on about just a few of Liverpool's ever-decreasing number of outstanding and historically significant pubs. Because of this some readers might still consider *Liverpool Pubs* to be incomplete. However, perhaps they will take this as encouragement to not only visit the places I have been able to include, but to explore for themselves those I have not.

Nothing of what I have written, though, would have been possible without the time and enthusiastic input of the pub licensees, managers, and staff who provided me with so much information. In the course of my exhaustive and taxing researches I was made very welcome in every hostelry I visited, and the willingness of these generous people to lubricate this process was much appreciated.

In particular, I would like to pass on my sincere gratitude and appreciation to the following people: Steve Hoy and Debbie Mousley at Ye Hole in Ye Wall; the bar staff at Thomas Rigby's; Jackie Friedlander and customers at The Poste House; Jimmy Williams at The Rose & Crown; David Hardman and Declan at The Lion Tavern; Kaye Nash and Eric Martyn at The Pig & Whistle; Mark Jervis at Ma Boyle's Oyster Bar; Kev Smith at The Cornmarket; Bar staff at The Cavern and The Grapes; Alfie and Jackie Buxton at The White Star; Paul Fitzgerald at The Liverpool ONE Bridewell; Simon Holt at The Baltic Fleet; David Coltman at The Monro; Bar staff at Alma de Cuba, and Rob Gutman, its founder and first proprietor; Iain Hoskins at Ma Egerton's Stage Door; Stewart Hemus, Marie Burns and Joyce McLinden at The Crown; Roy at The Vines; Arthur at Peter Kavanagh's; John O'Dowd at The Belvedere Hotel; Zardia Niaf, at Ye Cracke; Carol Ross at The Roscoe Head; Chris Mossop at The Philharmonic Dining Rooms; and Jacquie Richardson and Tony Nelson, at the Casa.

I would also like to thank staff and officers of Liverpool City Council, National Museums Liverpool, Liverpool Record Office, and the Liverpool Athenaeum Library, for so generously providing their time, expertise, and extensive knowledge.